By the Author of the best Latin Bo

Rave Herrera

Correct Stuttering

Discover the power to Transform your life

RAVE

The most sold

The Best Book to
Correct and
Overcome Stuttering

By

Santiago Rave Herrera

How to Correct Stuttering?

"Success is on the other side of fear"

"Always Great"

Dedicated to My Family and Geraldine because they always support me ...

Foreword:

I have closed a chapter in my life which I am very proud to have lived, I went through stuttering almost my entire life, I got over it and then I helped many people by becoming one of the people who has helped others the most in stuttering. It is nice to feel when you are part of a change in people, it is beautiful to know that despite having been a hard stage because the truth was not easy, I learned too much, I would live it again in another life if I were to be born again, because when you overcome the stuttering you realize that the most important thing is you and what you can contribute to others. Feeling important is fine, but feeling that you are worth to others is priceless.

My improvement began in 2016 and ended in 2017 after that, everything is happiness in my life, I would say that at 22 I began to be happy, the funny thing is that you do not become happy because you really overcome stuttering, you overcome yourself, stuttering is something anecdotal, it is simply the key to open a door that has been there, only that until now you have not been able to open it.

In the year 2021 I closed my chapter on everything that has to do with stuttering, I did not close it because I got tired, or out of boredom, or because of people, I close it because I already said everything, and this book is the closing of that beautiful novel that I'm sure will help you a lot. If you do everything that I will tell you: success and improvement is assured; What's more, my improvement was like when you travel with the car in constant mode without pressing the accelerator too much, that's the way it was, so if you want you can apply the accelerator, although the most important thing is consistency, no matter how fast you go, it will not matter either. how slow you go, the important thing is: never stop walking.

Thank you for having been part of this beautiful experience, thank you also for acquiring the book and giving me something that I am sure I will give you or at some point I will give you. I hope with all my heart that you live an unbeatable journey, that you enjoy this process, that you learn like never before, and that you never, never, never stop insisting, when you see yourself at the top it is easier to get there, when you visualize the path is simpler, therefore: always, always, always Great.

Thank you...
I love you so much!!

The Key to Change

Many people think that it is difficult to change, when change is simple, of course it is not easy, nowadays there is nothing easy, it is more ... nothing is easy, things are process, time and make you want (literal)

Although changes take time and are relative depending on the person, they are simple, others will think that a person of age is no longer possible to change, or that someone with such established roots either because they already have charcoal-grilled beliefs, but In a way this statement says that it is complex yes or yes, which kills any possibility of starting, imagine starting at a certain age with something you want and being told that it is going to be complex, or difficult, it is good to be realistic Sure, but when someone has stuttered a lifetime and you tell them that it will be difficult and that you are going to have to suffer because it doesn't motivate much, does it? In short, changes are possible when you really want to and you can see it in the mind materialized.

I had always been a supporter of the belief, that belief was everything, "that it was what made people go where they wanted to go" but ... as in many things there is a but ... after helping many people to overcome stuttering I I realized that the most important thing was not the belief but the "love" what the hell do I mean by this? : wanting something really makes your heart align with what you want, when you "want something" you look for a way to find it or many times it finds you and then you start to believe that it is possible. Wanting is much more important than believing, if you don't want to change it is very difficult, I put it that way honestly because what I want the most in this book is to be 100% honest with you: if you don't want to change, don't continue, literally, if you don't want to, the rest is stupid, you won't and you won't learn anything, why? Because you don't want a point.

Most of the people that I have helped or who have overcome stuttering alone have been because they have wanted to change, they have wanted to transform their lives, they are dissatisfied and already want a quick change, mmmm here is also something for you to consider Disagreement is not synonymous with change, but it helps a lot to know what it is that you don't want, and if you are dissatisfied, it is really easy to know that you do not want and that if you want, the problem is to remain dissatisfied, that is what most people do. , you've seen? People just deny and that's it, a clear example: in a soccer match one of the teams loses, the first thing the fans do is judge, kick the coach, the players, Raymundo and everyone else, they talk and talk how the game was, how bad the team played, but they don't give SOLUTIONS.

Although wanting is sometimes accompanied by nonconformity, it is more important to want from the constructive sphere, to want with desire, not to want with contempt, concluding this part a little, you can only overcome and correct stuttering if you want to do it, if in the Would you like it, if you yearn for that, if when you bought this book deep inside you felt that possibility, that is what moves the change. The belief in something can be an air donut, with this I do not mean that you do not believe, believe, it is important to believe, but the people who overcame it did not believe at first, because it is difficult, it costs, have you lived a lifetime like this and are you suddenly going to believe something different? Nooo because you need a process to build that belief of seeing the impossible possible, for now the key to change is wanting to change, not wanting to say, wanting to feel, remember this phrase and write it down for life, "Say you want doing it is very different from wanting to do it "

I'll tell you an anecdote that happened to me at work a while ago:

When I started looking for work after finishing university, I had to apply for several job interviews for architectural positions. When I applied to a company that I really liked, the owner of the company began to ask me the typical interview questions. I felt that I answered well the questions about the face that the owner asked me (although the truth I never knew if the person was pretending or it was true) in any case at the end of the interview there was a question that he asked me and it was: Santiago, do you think you can really apply for this position? He asked that question so seriously, as if he had not given a damn about what I had said before, at that moment I froze and didn't know what to say, I really didn't know if I could, so I said: "I think I can. I have what it takes for the position and I think I can do it. The man stared at me and said: ah, do you think? I immediately replied: no, no, no ... I can do it. I felt it was late, the man lowered his gaze and said: "Well, thank you very much Santiago, we will be calling you throughout the day to see if you are still in the process ... and blah ... blah ... blah, obviously during the day They did not call as usual, that day I learned something important: in the bottom of my heart I really did not want that company, moreover, I did not want any company, and that was noticed in the interview, at no time did I tell him: I want that position, then I understood that everything you want in the Life is more valuable than what you believe, because what you want you keep and what you believe you do not.

Debunking Some Myths

As in any field there are some myths that, although created by the same people or communities, other myths are created by science, yes! science, some will think that science does not believe myths or that the scientific guild is impure and always tells the truth, but let me tell you that over the years science has been wrong a lot, too much, it is normal, we are human beings and if science did not recognize its mistakes, I think progress would be difficult.

In this field of stuttering, myths abound too much, especially with science, why? That is the question! Because when there are no solutions, tests, measurements, especially research, what is resorted to is to say: -it is not known- or -mmmm it is something of the brain and that's it- The truth is that people do not know about this, again: why? Because it is not common, it is not easy, imagine thinking of someone who dedicates himself fully to stuttering, there are few people who do that, it is not common to see people who stutter, wait, maybe you tell me that it is common but it is because you have social networks, platforms, internet … etc … where you think there are many cases of stuttering, although there are many people in the world with stuttering, most of them are scattered out there. I agree that it is a very good population, although I mean that every day you do not find someone with stuttering, I say this because when many people have something in common science investigates more easily, in this case stuttering is not something so common that everyone has, we also know that it is complex, it is rare to understand, when you understand it people are in charge of inventing other things and that is where many do not know where to go or which is the true path of so many lies that there are .

When you enter the internet and put "stuttering" the searches appear in heaps: therapies, methods, remedies, exercises, an infinity of things that the truth is few and that you do not understand, because they are not based on logic. As I say: There is a lot of content out there, knowing how to discern is key if you want to find the true path, the good thing is that I am a person who has gone through all those rolls, if you have any doubts about stuttering, believe me I already lived it, for that when you try to read this book understand that its creator went through all the doubts you have, if there is something that I did not say here, believe me seriously, it was because it happened to me or it is not important to put it, as I said at the beginning I want this book to be simple , forceful and to the point.

Note: This book is not a stuttering book, it is a book to overcome and correct stuttering.

I want to make the note clear up there. In this book you will not find the different methods that exist for stuttering or what the high oligarchies think about stuttering, what treatises there are about this, what some foundations or the latest scientific advances say about stuttering, or also mention some therapies, mantras , and other pulls that believe me, with all my heart believe me that they are a waste of time, they are useless, have no logical foundation and lack any practical sense, what's more, imagine that I Santiago Rave Herrera I don't know how many methods there are of stuttering, I never studied them and I never cared, why? because it always came to the same thing, in any case you will understand later, maybe not now, but later yes, for now I would like to make it clear that this book is not an encyclopedia, it is not my life story, it is a book as a tool to overcome and correct stuttering: period.

There is a reflection that I want you to learn and it says: true knowledge is like friends: -scarce-. The people you will meet in life are a multitude, those who will remain there will be few, sometimes none, it is not that society is bad, things are scarce friend, that's why knowledge is worth it, you might think that the internet has everything If you have a lot of things, most of it, may that be of some use to you: little; really little, now the most complex: how do you know what works?

Once a guy spoke about the universe, he said that in the universe it is rare to find beings from other worlds, he made an example that when we take a glass and take water from the sea, the probability that a small fish is trapped there is scarce, really very scarce, but there are the fish, there are many, what happens is that there is more water than fish, so it is with the content: there is more useless content than useful.

Myths believe me that they will always continue to come out, maybe when you read this book, you reread it, internalize it, remain unhappy, you could say: this book is a myth, and you know something: it will be very good, if you believe that is your opinion and Each opinion is valid, but when you say that it is a myth I hope you can support it since that is where I do not think there is evidence to support it because this is the only way from my perspective in which there is no support or to be invalid.

The Myth of How Stuttering Arises

Understanding why things are created is important, to give you perspective, knowing how something arises can be comforting depending on the situations, for example, if someone has a pain it is good to know why it happened, or how it arose to understand how not to fall again In the same way, in other cases knowing how things arise is complicated because you would not know how, there are many factors, imagine that your foot hurts in a very specific area, you start to investigate what happened or where it was that you injured yourself or because that pain arose, you stay there for hours and hours thinking about the pain, is it really any use? Nooo (what you want is to relieve the pain) that it matters how the pain arose, it matters to fix it.

In stuttering, finding the origin is useless (literal), others will say yes or other things ... that's fine, but ask yourself what is the use of knowing how stuttering arose, I will tell you a little story:
A man named Marcelo was driving his car late at night, he was happily walking down the road towards his house, suddenly the tire of his bean bag car gets punctured, and the car begins to rake the pavement, Marcelo brakes abruptly and gets off of the car, he checks what has happened, looking closely he realizes that his tire is punctured by a nail, but Marcelo decided to go further because he had to solve the case, he checked the road very well if there were more nails, he found two more nails scattered , so the possibility arises that someone has played a joke on him or that someone out of evil has loosed the nails. Marcelo takes the car home and begins an exhaustive investigation, after a while they find the

suspect, put him in jail and Marcelo was happy until ... in a few years he looked at his garage again and the car still had a flat tire.

This story reflects how people with stuttering are left thinking about how stuttering arose in their lives, what was the trigger, what caused it, why to me? (typical question heard by everyone and that millions of people have said to do nothing)

What would have been really interesting about the story is that Marcelo realized that the tire was flat and sent it to be fixed - that's it - (what he needs is to fix the tire for God!) So do you You need a solution, you care how it came about if you can no longer change that, if things were solved like this, there would be no problems, don't you think? But okay, okay, let's suppose you want to do Marcelo's thing, you do a thorough investigation and discover that your great-great-grandfather had a stutter so the most common thing is to associate him with that person due to family traits, congratulations, you know why you stutter! mmm but it does help, hey ... is it done? Mmm right? Others say that it feels like a peace when you know the origin, I would not call it peace, remember that the mind plays with you, we will see it later, I call it conformists, as you already know where stuttering comes from, you already have a very good excuse for tell everyone the reason for this, let me tell you my dear friend that people don't care about that, your mind doesn't care either, what your mind wants is for you to stay the same because change requires thinking differently. Knowing where it came from could lead you to fall into that, to stay there, you are born, you grow up, they tell you that you cannot and you do not even try, becoming stagnant.

Nor do I say that it is bad that you do not investigate, do it, you have a free hand, hey ... after all it is your life and you will see, but it is worth staying around for so long in the same thing, most of the people who come to me the first thing They say is that: (which is... that... my parents... When I was little... .at my school I....when I was little I couldn't... .I think my grandmother had....) and so... typical stories; I understand the need to know, it is normal, we are human beings who want to understand everything, but believe me that staying there (which is the majority of people) is useless, everyone spends their life understanding things and not solving them, for example dreams, people spend more time on the limits that they are going to have than in dreaming that they can.

Excuses have that sweetness that reassures us, of course, it is a false sensation, the truth is we fill ourselves with dust, we break down filling ourselves with that ... excuses. If it is still not clear to you: -Quiet- let me tell you that I will give you an idea of how your stuttering arose so that you no longer keep hiding in excuses in case you are in those.

How stuttering is born

We know that there are two types of stuttering: The repetitive stuttering known as Clonic stuttering (co-co-co-heart) and the blocking stuttering known as Tonic Stuttering (Co… ..pause …… co… .pause…. Heart) Most people have both, which is known as mixed stuttering.

After this, science or people (especially people because they love to create mystery) said that there were more types of stuttering, that each person is different, that each stutter is independent and in a different way and blah, blah, blah … At the end you will realize in this book that the solution to stuttering is the same for everyone, because deep down we are very equal, yes, yes, we vary in personality, tastes, etc, etc, etc … but the way Our thinking is very equal unless you are an alien.

Many people or science does not know how it arises, but I will tell you this from my personal experience as a helper to thousands of people in this field.

Stuttering is very common that begins at an early age, many children at a young age begin to say the first syllables, hum things, join vowels, and develop the first words, in that period of time for some children it makes it more difficult than others, beginning to lengthen the words, to repeat them and to have to remove them with blocks to be able to say things. At this stage, many external factors can occur such as parents who demand their children with scolding, friends who laugh at the way they speak, relatives who ask the child to speak well, teachers … etc … The context that surrounds the child in this stage influences a lot, or other events may happen that mark the child with respect to speech.

When most children begin to speak they repeat words because they are forming them, they are structuring them, and there they begin to stutter, many of them pass this stage of stuttering as they are composing the words fluently and making compositions of sentences in a row, a few others become they remain stuttering generating "automatisms ---> that is, repetitions that remain embedded in the brain by habit" and speaking in this way: with pauses and repetitions, after acquiring these automatisms the context that surrounds the child and his mind begin to create that way of speaking.

Speech and body language gestures are created in the early stages of childhood, likewise the way of speaking is automatic, therefore, if the child creates these repetitions and blocks, his mind assimilates them as the way of express themselves and every time the days, weeks, months, years go by ... the child adopts that peculiar way of speaking called "stuttering"

This is the easiest way to understand how stuttering arises, obviously the way of speaking as I said at the beginning is influenced by the context, if the child begins to stutter and feels the fear of his parents for the way of speaking, the child begins to create those fears when speaking by generating more blocks and increasing repetitions, that is why fear, nerves and shyness make the child increase stuttering, for this reason people when they speak in public with fear they begin to stutter or block, for the simple reason that the mind is more focused on others, you feel the pressure not to make mistakes, you block yourself and each word comes out meaningless with incomprehensible repetitions, fear paralyzes you from an evolutionary perspective; When we are afraid our defense mechanism is to run away and we cannot process things, fear literally consumes you. In the same way, the context influences the child or the person who has stuttering, raising their stuttering to higher degrees, for that reason if you want to overcome stuttering you first need to start reflecting on the context, we will see this later.

So well, this is the most every day, logical and scientific way of acquiring stuttering, many people think that stuttering is born, which has no scientific or logical validity, stuttering as speech is constructed, children are not born speaking, certain children may have learning and memory problems, but that has more to do with genetic development, or also people who are born with difficulties within the speech apparatus (internal system that is responsible for producing the voice) that is already different Of course, many people excuse themselves in this, because since they do not understand why do they stutter? The first excuse is: it's something from the brain! My brain processes words very fast! (typical excuse heard everywhere) as a child my tongue was slow ... my mouth muscles are heavy ... things like that, etc ...

Most of the people I have treated do not have a scientific basis, medicated, proven, analyzed or with clinical studies that show that the person has stuttering for that reason, most are people without any type of medical problem, I did not say I don't think there is, of course there is, but the majority who come to me, if not all, are well both psychologically and clinically.

So ... I like this word ... do not think that stuttering is born with it, it just develops, and it is not something serious or for you to say: Ahhh, that's wrong, why did this happen !! .... etc .... Don't worry: -quiet- that's what we're here for, as I told you: there are many factors that cause you to have stuttering, and if you stay in the "Why?" You will not solve anything about things, do not be like Marcelo in the story, it is ridiculous to follow these steps, most people wonder why? but they never think "what for?

When I was little I consulted a lot about stuttering, I saw how by means of a statistic it said that, of every so many people, I think 1 million, only 2.02% had stuttering (those data were something like that at that time, no I know what statistic they are today) I was like WOW! It can't be, life shit on me (literal). What did I do to deserve this? Only 2% rays !! regrets ... regrets and regrets ... and of course !! The typical question Why me? I spent over 22 years thinking "why me?" to ask me "for what?" You have seen how when you ask yourself "why me" you do not solve anything, you see how you do not get out of there, it is as if you stayed in that question, why me? That's it, there is nothing more to do, it is as if you see life frustrated, after that question there is no more life to have.
The associations

He did not think to talk about this the truth, it is more it is one of the last themes that I finished writing. When I talk about associations, a very strange little juice enters my head, I can't finish finding flavor, it's like sweet at first, but in the end it turns bitter.

Nor do I want to understand myself in a bad way about the associations, I really like them with all my heart, I accept them, but I do not go with their policy, why? because in many cases it is useless, it serves to make the world understand that there is nothing else, although in some cases (few, very few) they do something for others.

Note: It must be said that lately the associations or institutions dedicated to stuttering are groups, companies, they are more dedicated to helping people rather than being a means to rejoice (that is good)

Why do I speak of "rejoice" or "shelter", because in many cases people find a comfort in these groups, it does not sound good to me, it is a comfort like feeling that there are more of the same people out there, that really is super good, but what comes after is something that is not right, and that is that when the person rejoices, a bubble is created by which, as he feels that he is different from the others, he always finds shelter in these associations.

Many of the associations are created as if it were a matter of politics that must be accepted in society, fight for human rights and ensure the acceptance of stutterers. Let me tell you, that is a great nonsense.

First of all, stutterers do not have to be accepted, or rejoiced, or treated as different people, apart, that is what is often promoted in associations. "How supposedly you speak badly then here you always have a place, we all support you, why? because you are ...... different "and the person listens to this and says:" ahiii yeah I'm different... "then he stays there in the associations and does nothing to change his life.

To change you have to roll up your sleeves, pants and start doing, you will never change because you are licking your wounds or feeling that you are part of a group which has to be accepted. Stutterers don't have to be accepted, they are already accepted!! The idea of not being accepted or fighting so that they have a place in society or so that people do not react in a bad way, or the many things that there are, is a blanket that they put on to feel that this happens.

Understand one thing, the world we live in is very relative, there are people who get married, there are people who separate, there are rich who remain poor, there are poor who remain rich, there are rich who are born rich, there are poor who remain poor, there are poor that are rich, etc.... You cannot assess all people with the same sword when it comes to being accepted by society, that is an idea that has no place, just as when people lament for being different, there is no need to lament for being different, you have to assert yourself for that which makes you different.

What most of these organizations do is: make you feel comfortable. You feel bad? don't feel bad, we're all like that here. I remember once of my great friend Luismi, one of my teachers, who was giving a lecture of which he showed a video that was: A boy who has a stutter invites several girls to dance with him, when he dances with several girls he starts talking with some of them but they laugh at him, others despair waiting for him to get the words out, but there is one who stares at him and says: -hey quiet, I'll give you time- and he stares at her, smiles and thinks : —Wow give me time— at the end of the video appears the logo of the association that promotes the video so that people: "give us time"

What do you think of the story I told you? It really sounds nice, it is sweet, but if you look at it carefully, it is not as sweet as it seems, "it is a camouflage" at first you will think that you should be accepted or that people should give you time, but people will not do that, if the people do it, you will create an idea that this is the way it should be, deep down you will be relegating your power to people because you will always depend on what others approve or not. That is the point I wanted to get to. The associations are more aimed at what others think of stutterers than what the stutterer thinks, everything is based on external people, the "normal" assumptions

I am going to give you an example that I will also relate later, but it is so that you know why the idea of associations is poorly focused.

Imagine a world where everyone is a stutterer, all the people on the face of the earth are stutterers, the years go by and people who do not stutter but who speak "fluently" are coming out, these people will think that they are different from everyone, that they do not stutter. The rest of the people who stutter see them strange, why? because it is not something common, obvious, so fluent people will feel rejected and start to find Rare more fluid people, then they group together and since they feel they are rejected by society they demand to be accepted, then they create an organization called the "fluentitis" these promote fluidity, demand rights, look different and want to have a place in the world (you sounds familiar)

As I said at the beginning, associations are not really bad, it is the approach that is given, associations are important when you find other people from whom to share experiences, when you find support to overcome yourself not to rejoice, when you find people like you with the idea of doing great things, that vibrate in the same tune, the rest what an association can tell you is very measured since these are based a lot on staying in the comfort zone.Have you ever wondered why people do not exceed the stuttering with associations? Exactly because it is a pure comfort zone, what I recommend is that you find people there to share, nothing more, remember something that you will understand when you finish the process, stuttering is an individual process, why? because it is something that has to do with you, you with you, you with you.

Another of the last things that I will tell you about this is: There are many people with broad positions in the associations, groups that tell you that through techniques, methods, hypnosis, stuttering is overcome, or simply people with their such "methods." what causes many times is blur, if you saw the number of people who come to me with those ideas and then end up releasing all that, because those things do not work, pure blur, you start a process like this that is proven, grounded, with experience , testimonials, etc... .etc... etc... for trying to make such a method of someone who has no idea what stuttering is and even less

27

that it has not helped anyone. This is where one has to choose the right path.

Overcoming & Correction

Overcoming and Correction are very different things and I want you to be very clear about it, since hereinafter we are going to be using these terms so that you become familiar. It is very simple and I want to give you an example:

When you buy a computer, this is a machine that has a keyboard, screen, speakers, mouse, as well as all those physical components that are known as the "hardware" when you turn on the computer we enter into its brain to which we can put programs , games, entering the internet and all that world happens inside the brain of the computer, this is commonly called "software". The same thing happens with us human beings, especially with our language, on the one hand our brain is in charge of process words, letters, messages, organize them, think, and on the other hand our mouth, larynx, muscles, and all that set of organs that is known as the speech apparatus is the one in charge of getting those words out and making them tangible.

So well, stuttering is divided into two parts, the "Mentality" which is our thoughts, our software and the other part is the linguistics which is our physical part, what is tangible, our "voice", the sound we make, the modulation that we do with the mouth, all that is the hardware. When we talk about Overcoming we will talk about the mental part, and when we talk about Correction we will talk about speech as such, in conclusion, Overcoming has to do with the Mind and Correction with Speech is already there.

Overcoming -------------- Software --------- Mindset / Brain

Correction ---------------- hardware ------- Voice, Muscles / speech apparatus

Why is it important to divide it? You might ask. The truth is that this does not matter, what happens is that if you have clear concepts it will be very easy for you to understand how everything happens structurally and because this "Change" has logic, it is scientific and it is something that cannot be discussed, because as I told you At the beginning there will be many doubts, schools, hypotheses about this, or people who tell you about stuttering, but what I will tell you makes sense and the best of all is REAL.

Note: Have you seen that I really like the notes? There is a little thing that I would like to make clear, when I say that something is scientific, I mean that it has a basis based on science, that it is rational, such as the earth is round and not flat, that is already based on science. can see from space, there are many photos of the earth. The same thing happens when I talk about stuttering, not only do I put my experience, I put that of many and thousands of people who went through the process with me and thousands of others who went through the same process without me. When I spoke previously about science it is different, since I mean that science as a branch does not understand stuttering, because it is complex, it is not encouraged, because maybe nobody pays to do a deep investigation of the subject, but not I want to say that science is bad, therefore, it is excellent, only that in many cases it has been wrong, but ... and closing this note, when I speak of a scientist I mean that it has solid, firm bases, testimonies and many real arguments that They support him, for example the earth is round and not flat, so I am not referring to science as a branch but to the solid bases that support a statement.

The overcoming

Every first change in our life is born from our thoughts that is linked to feelings and all that that we will see later, but in the first stage the change is born by our mind. Most people are wrong thinking that changes are born by situations, by moments, by people or something external, and let me honestly tell you that this book will not change your life. Here you will think that it is a waste to continue reading this book, or why did you buy it, but wait !! WAIT !! That is good, it is the best there is, life cannot make you change because if it were like that you would be a puppet, you would be a slave of the external. The only person who can make you change is yourself, you here will think: well, the same thing again, how can you affirm that? Let me tell you this story:

You are here reading these words, you see how you are reading, you think that I am saying this to you in some way, in your head when you read these words you think that I am the one who is saying them, but in reality you are the one who interprets these words and you give it a value, maybe when you read this you say: —ahiii what a fool this guy says— or you say —wow how interesting— either of the two positions does not make any sense, you will always be the one at the end that gives value to what you read: it's good, I like it, I don't like it, interesting, horrible, etc. When we remember a deceased person we do not really remember the deceased person, we remember what we think of that person who has left. I know these things sound a bit philosophical, and my intention is not to make you think about the existentialism of life or to make a mental circuit in your brain, my intention is that you can see reality, what is REAL.

Imagine that you come home thinking about a person you don't like, you think, think and think. Several days pass and unfortunately you meet that person, at this point it is important that you stop to think about what happens when you see that person. The first thing that happens is that thoughts of that person arrive, the thoughts do not really arrive, they arise from you to see that person, those thoughts that arise are interpretations that you have of that person, after those thoughts arise you charge yourself with a certain type reaction, in this case it may be a bad reaction because you don't like that person, the first thing we all do is: hang on to those thoughts, ride with them, we believe that idea. But, always -but- this is where something important is concluded: if the thoughts you have arise from you about that person, those thoughts are yours and what you see in front is not really the person, what you see is: ¡¡¡ AN INTERPRETATION OF THAT PERSON !! CLAROOOO !!! You see what you think of her.

I just said all that stream to make it clear that everything that arises in life are your interpretations. As everything is your interpretations, you are the only one who can change them, nobody else, learn this that will be important in this process as well as for your life:

"You are not the author of what happens in the world, but you are the author of how you interpret the world"

If you propose to control the world, it will be a utopia, because everything happens without you being there, but everything that happens around you is your responsibility for how you interpret it. The same happens with overcoming, people do not overcome by external situations, by books, by mantras, people overcome because their interpretations change. If you believe that the external makes you change, you are highly manipulable, because whatever they paint you, you will let yourself be carried away by that, people do not change through a book, people change through books; when the same people read, they themselves change their way of thinking, they themselves !! --------------------------- ---> REMEMBER.

I understand that people give value to things, to what they do, to life itself, that is really beautiful, it is something that is typical of the human being, giving a certain sweetness, power, energy, positivism, among others to what It happens to us every day or what we have, but life has no meaning, it does not have that roll that human beings give it and it has no power to make you change.

The only power in the world to change is you, having this clear makes you take control. Do not give power to things, to the external, much less to something that will not continue with you when you are gone. The family is beautiful, the people around you are very cool, but they won't bury you on the day of your death, why? because that is not their life, everyone has their life, yes, yes, we are social people, that is more than clear, but the mind as your life is managed by you, that is why you have the power to do whatever gives you the gift wins, I don't want to sound motivating, I want to be realistic.

That is why overcoming is born from you through this book, do not give me the power, do not give the power to this book, give yourself the power, because it has always been with you.

Returning to the initial point, overcoming stuttering is born from mental change, what we think about what happens to us. When we talk about overcoming we will talk about the mentality, I warn you that almost 80% of this book is about the mentality. Why? I like this question besides that I can give you a thousand reasons to defend what I tell you, because if you want, listen to me very well, if you want to overcome stuttering to have an incredible life you can only do it from the mental side, THERE IS NO OTHER WAY (----- RELITERAL ---) to all the people that I have treated as those who not only overcome stuttering by the Mental Path.

The Correction

It really shouldn't be called correction; When we talk about correction we talk about having to change something because it is wrong, correcting comes from school, when we were wrong and the teacher told us that it was wrong, that we had to "correct it" The truth is that in life there is nothing to correct, there are things to look at.

What do I mean by this: when we correct something we do not correct it because it is wrong, we correct it because we "think" that it is not like that or because society determines it, in life there is nothing bad, good or to improve, life It is as it is expressed on a daily basis, we take care of giving it a value or judging such a thing. For that reason, seeing stuttering as something that needs to be corrected is not good posture, moreover, it is something that can slow the process if you look at it that way, learn this: in life there are no problems, there are situations for face, more than situations to face, there are situations to SEE !! Because when you see --- -> you understand, when you understand you have already understood naturalness and naturalness implies being realistic.

Note: Being realistic is having your feet on the ground looking towards what you want to achieve, being realistic is being logical.

The word "correction" is really used for marketing, I know it sounds strange to say this, but if I called the book: Improve your stuttering or Evolve your stuttering, I would not pull anything, nor would anyone want to acquire it, calling it correction makes people want to be more interested Remember that my goal is to be completely honest with you.

Well, after having clarified this, the correction could be called evolution, when you go from stuttering to flow you don't really correct, you stop doing something you were doing for something different, you evolve.

34

"A flower when it blooms does not bloom because it judges what it is before it blooms, it simply blooms because it evolves"

The same happens with stuttering, you never correct the stuttering because you have nothing to correct, the stuttering was created by you, how could you judge that? You just go to a new stage. Seeing it this way makes you feel that everything is a process, it becomes real, you never climb a mountain thinking that the first steps should not be done, you climb the mountain thinking that you have to take the first steps to get there, everything has a cycle in the life, just as when you achieve something, you achieve it by having started, the whole process is fruit, defeats or failures are approaches to success.

Likewise, we will continue to call it correction hahahahaha for ease of understanding, but you already know what correction we mean, okay. As I mentioned at the beginning: you created stuttering and it is very good, but very good, it is to really applaud, I mean it with all sincerity, now you may think that it is crazy…. then you will give me the reason.

Everything in life needs praxis, what is known as practice, "practice makes perfect" you have surely heard this everywhere, always remember this: when a phrase becomes cliché: (referring to something that is heard many times) for something will be. The human being cannot detach himself from the practice, even today we do not have the ability to change something external only through our mind, I say for now of course, then who the hell knows, if you want to ride a cycle you will need to practice to learn, or play the piano, play a sport, anything needs practice, even the mind itself needs practice, note that even meditation requires practice, when you start to meditate you don't really meditate, you get crazy thoughts, and you let yourself be carried away by pure earthly thoughts When you practice daily you meditate in tranquility.

Surely you have heard another saying that says: From said to fact there is a long way. Words like thoughts remain in the air, materializing ideas requires practice, what I mean by this so that we can focus more is: Just as you created stuttering day after day with daily practice, you also have to start speaking fluently with daily practice. At this point you may say:

but I didn't practice stuttering! I'll tell you: Sure you did! you just weren't aware of it! Day after day you spoke, you said words, you hit them, the context influenced and everything that was said before, day after day you built it, later we will see a little more of this, but I would like to make it clear that everything in life is practical.

Now ... what is practice?

Practice in a few words is synonymous with process, learn this because I will repeat it many times: | The process is everything |

I left it separate and bold so you can find it easy if you ever doubt what we are doing. Process is what makes mastery to be achieved, when you acquire any skill, you acquire it by pure process, because you do the same thing every day. Grab something you have there on hand, anything for Please, you got it easy right? Sure you didn't even think to grab it, it was easy I imagine, but if you didn't have that ability to grab things, would it be easy for you? Would you do it so fast? ... the truth is that it would take a while, you would have to do it daily to develop the ability to grasp as easy as you do now, if you tell someone who has regained mobility in the hand it would be difficult grab something, things would fall off, it would be like a child starting to move his fingers, only until he does it several times it will not be easy.

Now imagine that throughout your life you never used your tongue to speak, and now you start to use it, you would speak more tangled than a mop (literal) you would not even know how to say a word, you would have to start learning to speak, that's my good friend requires two points: "process"

There are several myths about the process that we will see well later, being clear that to begin to flow it is necessary practice, at this moment everything is light pink, although ... as you already have a way of speaking installed, it needs a process a bit more demanding, I do not mean difficult, nor complex, because the truth is not, only that the process with stuttering is a little more demanding, that's good because as you demand yourself you see results, I am in favor of the results being What motivates the most is like when a soccer team loses games in a row, what motivation can it have? Some will say: you learn from mistakes, yes, but it is more beautiful to learn when you win the matches, I understand that learning is reflected more from the mistake, but by winning you learn to win, when you win-win-win you learn to win , life is not many times as they told you you know, you have to have a head not to swallow what others tell you.

In stuttering you have a way of speaking that is yours, you built it, that way of speaking is a habit that making it change as I told you well requires a little more process, I would like to tell you this reflection, it is an analogy of a Confucius phrase :

"Habits come as passengers, visit us as guests and remain as masters"

Letting go of a habit does not happen overnight, letting go of a habit requires again: process. The way you speak is a habit that is roasted over charcoal but that through practice will be transformed, that is why it is so important to know how to "relearn" learning does everyone, it is easy to learn something, but relearning costs a little more, it requires more work, because as you already have a way of speaking installed, letting it go is harder, that is why people who unlearn have a high capacity to adapt to change. If you think about it, human beings have been a kind of habits but that over time they have had to unlearn, otherwise the human being would never have survived since they could not adapt to changes and these changes would eat them alive.

Today we live in a world where everything runs, is fast, moves thousands and thousands of seconds, information flies, everything is flash ----- wait ------ don't get carried away by that, because the The world goes a thousand does not mean that you will have to go a thousand and adapt immediately, I know that the changes are to hit everything, before that you have to have PATIENCE.

To conclude this part, the correction as we will continue to call it is focused on "daily practice" in a few words is "relearning again" let me tell you a true story:

A woman named Riona Kelly was paralyzed from the waist to the feet as she suffered a stroke, the doctors told her that she would never walk again, that the truth would take a lot of work. She was devastated, especially because her husband, who had been married for years, asked for a divorce from her.

Time passed and she met a former rugby player named Keith Mason who told her that she might be able to rehab and walk again. They set out to train hard. They constantly did therapies to strengthen her legs, although she commented that at first she practically dragged her body with no sign that her legs were going to respond, but that she still continued.

Every day she increased her strength both mentally and physically until she gradually through many therapies she began to walk.

This is a small true story of many that shows us how when we propose something we can achieve it, but beyond proposing ourselves: there is doing, practicing, persisting and not giving up, the "process" ------- > Did I tell you what is most important?

If you plan to flow in a perfect way you will achieve it with process (literal) because the daily process makes you a MASTER.

So to conclude the correction that we are going to see are a series of actions that you will be doing daily, I do not want to anticipate you because first there are certain things that you should know.

The vision

This is an important rudder within self-improvement.

Note: Thank you for following my dear and great friend, this is what will make you send where you want to go.

When you propose to do something, it is not enough just to do it, it takes more, we have talked about wanting to do things, but if you want something, how do you know where to row?

When we want something we want it and our doubt enters, where do I go? Knowing where you are going makes all energies focus there. The sages say that purpose is when you align your thoughts, feelings and actions towards one direction, that's true you know! When you have a goal you arrive because you arrive, because anything can happen, the world can fall, but if you have to move a mountain to get there you move it, having the goal makes the path irrelevant, no matter where you start, many people are left with the question of: Tell me how do I do it? Where do I begin? When do I take the first step? BULLSHIT !! Pussy start !! It just starts, the stones settle on the road, when you know where to go you don't ask yourself those blowjobs, I understand that it is normal, I understand it, you will see, but ... the truth is that you have to have a GOAL.

Vision is purpose, that which makes you move, that makes you get up, if you don't know what you get up for every day you don't know what you live for. Many people who came to me asked them why they wanted to overcome stuttering, many told me that they wanted it to feel good with their friends, family, colleagues, etc ... most of them said that to me, I understand the beauty of wanting to speak better, or whatever it's called, of wanting to be accepted by others, but that goal is very sad, you know, the few people that I managed when their vision was bigger than them, they overcame it easier.

When I overcame stuttering, my vision was not to be accepted by others or speak well and feel "comfortable :(" noooo !!!, my vision was to be able to become one of the greatest "Coaches" that the company has ever given. humanity, my vision was to give talks all over the world, train people, motivate masses of people, communicate valuable words to people, inspire millions of people, that is vision, vision is something that goes beyond heaven. Remember:

"Always aspire to touch the sky, even if you stay in the clouds"

The desire that you are going to put into a big goal does not compare with the desire that you will put into a small goal.

There is a key in motivation that is called Cost X Benefit, this means that the higher the benefit you have, the lower the cost you will have to do and the lower the benefit you have, the higher the cost you will do. This in a few words means that if you set a high goal, the cost that you will see reflected, you will not notice it because you know that something great will come, because you know that the main course is exquisite, but ... if you have a goal "chichi" the cost will be very high, you will feel that you are trying a lot, you will get tired and put everything aside.

"The greatest danger for us is not that our goal is high and we do not reach it, but that our goal is so small and we reach it" Miguel Ángel Buonarroti

A very everyday example that is used a lot in sport is the following: Several athletes participate in a national athlete race, the prize is a cup. Athletes train day, afternoon, night, but they train without enthusiasm since the achievement is a cup, really nothing motivating, others do not train, the process is lost. In another scenario we have a career of international athletes in which several athletes participate, the prize is to be a world winner of athletics, plus everything that this recognition implies and the sum of great money. Athletes train with great pride, with enthusiasm, they know that reaching the top will be historic, day by day they train very hard to win, they know that the rival is training harder so they increase their level of training, for a day Those who don't train get frustrated, hard and constant training is the key for the best athlete to win.

When you are on the road to improvement and you feel a lot of effort to get there or you are about to give up, do not throw in the towel, always review the goal, because in most cases it has to do with the goal you set for yourself. On the other hand, if you have a clear and motivating goal and at some point in the process you get frustrated, depressed or lost, do not change the goal, change the plan, but never change the goal, since what keeps you stuck there is the goal. . In this you will have to be very attentive to how you move along the path.

The Arguments and the Facts

As we had already said at the beginning, stuttering is divided between the improvement that has to do with the mental part and the correction with the linguistic part or speech as such. If we think about the mentality is very open, as well as the speech, what I mean is that you could do many things in the mental and speech part but none would guarantee you progress, how like that? If I tell you that overcoming has to do with the mental, you will wonder if mentally you need new ideas, hypnosis, meditation, change of perspectives, many other things because the mentality is very open, as well as speech, you might think that then in the correction you would have to do breaths, tongue twisters, exercises, etc ... I am not saying that all this is useless, what I am saying is that it will not show results, it will be something in the long term, besides that many of the things do not go focused on the problem as such.

Imagine that you want to kill a fly that is in the whole house, you can take a grenade and throw it and yes you will kill it, but you will destroy the house, was that worth it? Is efficient? I give you another more specific case: imagine that you want to learn English so you start by learning the most complex words in English with the idea that by learning complex words you will be able to master English, really? That would take years, maybe not, but if it will be more complicated, the ideal would be to learn the words, phrases and everyday communications, since that way you would understand what others are saying more easily and you could defend yourself by communicating a little.

I'm going to give you two other cases so that this is very clear. I place a lot of emphasis on this. When I helped people directly in the process of improvement, some asked me if what I was telling them really worked, some obviously doubted (although later in time they no longer doubted to see the results) when some of these doubted they told me that if they could do others things besides what I told them, I told them in a good way that they were free to do what they wanted. The funny thing is that later they came to me saying that I was right, that they were "blurring" of course !! When you do many things you never focus, why do so many things if you can do the most important thing and now. "When you do the RELEVANT, the irrelevant accommodates itself"

There is a rule that is used for people who live loaded with work, it is called the 80/20 rule, what this rule means is: when you have many things to do you must understand that you will not be able to do them all, the most important thing is to do the urgent, that which is the fundamental thing is 20% of everything you have to do, if you do that 20% very well the other does not matter, there are things that will come out alone and there are others that you simply will not do and nothing happens . The stones settle on the path remember. The 80/20 rule is applied by many successful entrepreneurs, because they know that they cannot do all things, just by doing 20% of what they have to do or what is urgent or important is everything. It is hard to believe this rule, but if you apply it not only in overcoming stuttering you will see great results believe me.

Has it ever happened to you that when you try to do everything you don't end up doing anything, or when you start a task and jump to another you think: —It seems that it took me longer— The truth is that the brain also behaves that way, doing multitasking or several tasks at the same time our brain gets tired, stressed, it is strange to think that, but yes! Our brain gets stressed! Ideally, do one task at a time.

It is also likely that the typical case has happened to you when you change something in your life, that change affects everything, in the end you end up saying: "Whoa, whoa, whoa, I didn't think that was so important." Everything was transformed from what you changed, the problem many times is that human beings forget that it was the change we made, we do not realize it and that is why we relapse into the same thing (typical of stuttering, many come saying that in some During the time of their life they felt good but now they do not know why they relapsed. Others say: I recently felt in the clouds and I want to reach that state, but I do not know what happened to me at that time)

Focus, focus, focus ... I am going to give you an everyday example: Imagine that I give you a puzzle, it is a very complex puzzle that has a man's face on a background that is all blue, when you start to put it together you realize that all the tiles on the blue background are the same, you start to think that it will be very complex to start with the blue tiles (but... you light up) you think that the most ideal thing is to start with the man's face because that way it is simpler, you arm the face of the The man and the other pieces in the background are assembled by having the face of the armed man.

Focus, focus, focus ... When you learn to drive a car, or if you haven't learned, the first thing they teach you is where to drive from Ha the car, where is the steering wheel, the brake, the accelerator pedal, put parking lights, how to put the turn signals, all that. You think they will show you where the engine is, what components a car has, where the nut that joins the wheel gear with the rear wheels is, NOOOO they don't teach you that. Why? because it doesn't matter: -period- the only thing that matters is that you know how to drive the car, that's it -period-

The same thing happens with stuttering, many deep down what they want are concepts, to know what stuttering is made of, the parts, how it is divided, things that do not work, all that sucks! you are interested in knowing what language development is like at a certain age for the clonic type of stuttering, WTF! So that? the important thing is to evolve, not to know how the evolutionary development was, I repeat: I'm not saying don't do it, do it! Maybe it won't do any good, you may think that yes, well ... then you'll agree with me, as I said at the beginning, I've been treating people with stuttering for longer than anyone else, so I already know them all, I don't want to sound egocentric either, what happens is that sometimes you have to show reality so that people do not take you as a patch, but know and understand that for something I say things.

All that said (I feel a bit the anger above) it is time to tell you the most important thing in Overcoming and Correcting.

The most important thing is the Arguments and the Facts. The arguments are thoughts that you are going to create to give yourself mental strength, in a few words they are thoughts that you are going to believe little by little to build a new perspective (if you have not understood it now, calm down) we will see it later with an example; the arguments have to do with Overcoming Do you know why? You should know by now, because it is about the mind.

The facts are actions that you are going to create to give reason to the arguments, in a few words the facts are habits that you will do daily to reinforce the arguments, because the facts in the end is what will give you the fastest results, what you It will allow us to understand reality and what will make what you have been arguing materialize. The facts reinforce the mindset and correctness. (here if you do not understand it calmly, you will understand it with the examples) at the end I will leave a developed case of a person and my personal experience (so do not worry about the concepts)

Let's take a real everyday example: We know that most people believe in some religion, process some Faith or have some God. If we analyze in detail respectfully clear, we will realize that the belief of a certain religion is a belief as its name indicates, behind what people profess there is a belief: "Is the person believing in something" if we are clear up to that point we We will find that creating a belief requires arguments and facts. A person who believes in a religion is someone who, from a young age or for a certain time, has created arguments why that religion is the most important, some may argue about cases of miracles they have witnessed, others because their parents taught them to do so. It was the religion that they believed, others because they feel that believing in that religion makes them free, etc, etc, etc ... People argue why they believe, if you ask someone who processes faith why does he believe? He will give you a series of arguments as to why he believes in the religion he claims to believe, if you are about to tell him that that religion is not true, or that it is a lie, the person will defend his religion with arguments, he may tell you: I as a child I have believed.... once I could not find meaning in life.... and I rejoiced in this religion and it has given me everything I ever wanted.... once my family was ill and through prayers they have always been healthy ... etc ... everything the person says are arguments that affirm her belief.

Now, someone who believes not only believes by arguments, but also demonstrates it with facts, so the majority of people who really profess a faith are people who daily go to monasteries, say prayers, make prayers, attend related events, keep the word. , they do facts, which increasingly reaffirm the belief.

When a child is born, his parents usually teach him the religion to which he must believe, the child does not understand this very well but as he grows up he feeds on content, sentences, arguments, reflections, what he sees is feeding his arguments as to why that religion is the one to follow, when he is older, he may argue everything that happens to him, for example: if he is almost run over by a car, the young man will say: "Wow!" thanks to such a religion I have been saved. Then he hears how his aunt had cancer that later disappeared by a divine miracle, or he meets with his family from time to time to say prayers, all this fuels the belief, then the young man begins to adopt that same position: he performs r prayers, songs, prayers, etc. Every time the boy does this he affirms more and more his religion, he creates strong columns. It is very unlikely that someone would come and give him another point of view by making the young man change his mind, it is rare that, rather what the young man will do is reject him arguing that the religion in which he believes is the truth.

This is how most people acquire a belief, be it religious or otherwise. The belief is confirmed with arguments and facts, a biblical phrase said that the word became flesh, and it is the truth you know, what you say you end up materializing, to each thought there is a reaction.

Stuttering is the same thing that was said before, as a child it is likely that you were arguing about things about stuttering, people, others, what could happen if you stuttered, what they could think if you got stuck in words, through actions such as hiding, feeling rejected, not participating, staying silent, not being in meetings because of having to expose yourself, not talking to such a person, all those actions made you now have a concept about the stuttering and a mentality about stuttering, whether it benefits you or harms you, in most cases are beliefs that harm you of course, or you would not have bought this book, maybe you bought it for rubber, maybe hahahaha, well ...

The point is that ... just as you have that structure of stuttering, it is also how you have to deconstruct it, if I told you that stuttering is something positive that has come into your life so that you can improve yourself as a person, you will tell me that this is a stupidity because stuttering is something horrible, that does not allow you this, the other, that, what about, that no, blah, blah, blah ... ... you will tell me arguments about what you think about stuttering (I understand it, from You will see that I understand) that does not justify that it is real, that it is true, it is only your arguments, opinions or beliefs about what you have.

I already warn you of one that the process that we will do has to do with this, you know, why? Because changes come through arguments and facts, no one in life changes a way of thinking by chance or because a little bird came to tell him ... the changes happen because the person is about to change through the ... PROCESS !! Thatoo !! Process!! Before this I will tell you something about beliefs.

The Beliefs

Beliefs are ideas that we have grilled over charcoal, when I say grilled on charcoal I mean that these ideas are stamped on us as we have been cultivating them since we were small or grown up.

I will leave you this reflection that is part of the whole process that we will have:

"Cultivate a thought and you will cultivate an action, cultivate an action and you will cultivate a habit, cultivate a habit and you will cultivate a lifestyle"

The above I left it bold and highlighted because it is practically what makes you change your life completely. When we talk about overcoming we are not talking about stuttering and now, we are talking about your life, you and I know that stuttering now governs your life in many aspects not to mention everything. -I get it, it's normal. In my case, not even painting rules my life, I rule her obviously, but don't worry, you will reach this level as soon as we finish this process, which will be fast if you do everything I tell you.

I will tell you a certain metaphor so you can see how interesting beliefs are:

Imagine that you have a completely empty glass, that empty glass is your mind as a child, when you grow to that glass you put a red liquid, that red liquid is the thoughts, ideas, words that the people around you are instilling in you, such as family, colleagues, friends ... every time one of these people tells you that stuttering is horrible, you fill the glass with red liquid. Each time you grow, you fill it more, the more it fills, the more the red liquid settles (you will think that when time passes that red liquid will tend to change) but what the research says is that as you get older you reinforce your beliefs, as well as your personality, which means that the longer that red liquid passes, the redder it becomes so to speak. Now what is important? Most of the people are floating in that red liquid and do not know how to get out of there, or where to start, what many do is think that they can throw the red liquid, that is very silly. Think for a second what would happen if you empty your mind, after emptying it your mind will look for a way to fill it again ------- what do you think it will fill the glass with? ------> Exactly! = with red liquid.

The fundamental thing to leave the red liquid is to "realize" Sure! Realizing that swimming in the red liquid is useless, it hurts you more, it is old liquid, it is settled, it is no longer useful, it is obsolete, the most important thing is that it makes you feel bad. Another thing would be if the red liquid makes you feel good, although it is a game of the mind many times to think that everything is fine, when deep down things are going very badly.

Note: Many people came to me to treat them, when I treated them they told me that everything was fine, that they knew how to handle stuttering, that the truth was that what happened was something small, going deeper I realized that it was not Thus, he showed it to the person and he realized that his life was full of spiders that hid what was really happening.

It is everyday that people fail to understand their lives, because it is of masters to take an internal look. There is a reflection that a great teacher of mine shared with me in my overcoming stuttering and I want to share it with you:

"Many people think they know what they are like, but they really don't know that they don't know what they are like"

The typical thing for many people is to think that they really know each other when what they think they do not even know how to control.

Returning with the glass full of red liquid, now it is time to think: how on earth do I do to remove the liquid? We know you can't throw it away, so what can you do? The most logical thing is: replace it! Of course! This is why I like to be realistic! If you want to change beliefs you have to replace them yes or yes.

When we pour a liquid into the glass full of red liquid, it must be done slowly, gently, but always continuously, when you pour the new liquid over the red liquid you will begin to notice that the red liquid is coming out little by little and this is how the new ones beliefs are replacing old beliefs.

It is easy to tell it, it does not mean that it is difficult to do it, it is how I will always repeat the "process" as well as how you built those beliefs grilled over charcoal and you will have to incubate the new beliefs that will transform your life, remember the reflection:

Sow a thought and you will reap ...

The Responsability

When we talk about responsibility we do not talk about the responsibility that they teach us at school or at home, that responsibility is stupid the truth (literally, that would give for another book) the responsibility we talk about is about your life, you with you, with you towards you , you with life, you with your being.

You will wonder why the importance of this topic, let me tell you that all the topics that I will put here I put them because of the high importance, everything you see in this book is fundamental, even the reflections if you have them very clear you will be able to keep them in mind throughout the progress.

Look, if I tell you something important that seems minimal, a well-thought-out sentence is capable of making you change so quickly that you won't even realize when it was. I leave you this information: the majority of people who have achieved in their life what they have wanted have always started from a maxim (understood as a phrase, a saying, a message) so no matter how silly a reflection is capable of make you get the best version of you, but ask Hitler when he thought that the Germans were pure blood.

Continuing with the responsibility (I know that sometimes it seems that I deviate from the subject as now hahahaha but it is so that things become clear) I open parentheses again (deep down you know that they are important, I close parentheses) we had said that this responsibility has to see with your life, it is very likely that when something happens we will look for a culprit immediately, it is our nature, we do not want to be the fool of the movie, much less, we want to look good for an evolutionary issue, although the reality is that everything that What happens in life is your responsibility, it may not be like that, you see, it may be people who are responsible, but it is better to see it that way, why? because it's easier to manage life from your perspective, although I don't like the word manage, let's call it observing, that's why I'll tell you an anecdote:

Marta was a woman who lived very quietly at home, at Christmas she was in charge of making the house very beautiful, everyone who passed by admired Marta's house from the window. Every Christmas Marta was the sensation because of the way she fixed the house. People always passing by stopped at the house, took photos, looked at the inside of the house and many gathered to gossip about the house. Time passed and Marta was very bothered by how people broke into her privacy, but what could she do? She loved Christmas for her family, she couldn't take people out every so often, and her house was in an area where a lot of people walked. Time passed and people no longer looked at the house, everyone who passed by said: Wow! What a horrible house! Was this the beautiful Christmas house? There is nothing left ... many said ... but ... What had happened? Marta had not cleaned the window glass again and everyone who passed by thought that the house was dirty because they saw through the foggy window, but inside the house it was still the most beautiful house at Christmas.

This little story tells us how important it is to look through your window. Most people look through the window of others, if you look through the window of others it gives you a totally different perspective of reality, that's why I like to be ... Realistic ...

The responsibility of your life is something that you have in your hands, living life with that makes you have the power, that is why we said at the beginning never give the power to something external because you will be highly manipulable, always give yourself the power to You, let's dig a little deeper into this on stuttering.

First of all, there is a statement that is real and it is: "You are solely responsible for having brought about stuttering" having this clear frees you from prejudices, not being clear about this you suffer, period.

Knowing that you have stuttered is very good, excellent !!! It's to applaud, it's super good, NOTHING HAPPENS, it's very good, you brought it into your life as a child, you fed it with what others said, you watered it as if it were a plant each and every one of your days and now it you have established in you and it is - super good !! It's a note !! - You really do! Because that is what makes you what you are today! And let me tell you my friend that you are incredible and not because I say so but because to live you need much more than a matter of luck, it is almost impossible for you to be there where you are, all that had to happen for you to be reading this book is amazing, everything so connected, precise, perfect, this moment while reading these words is phenomenal. Thank you and infinite thanks for existing.

There are many people who come to me and the first thing they tell me is: that their parents were the culprits, or their brothers, or their friends, there is always someone out there that caused them to stutter (:(:(:() stay you In that perspective it is useless, although if it was That, something that is not so clear, it would not help you either, imagine that your parents as a child told you not to stutter that that sounded very ugly, that you speak well, that stuttering is for the weak or things like that, now you are what you are for giving validity to all those blowjobs (sorry for the expressions but I like to get to the point) Living life blaming people makes you empower them. When you were little you were easy to mold because you were a child and you let yourself be carried away, now you grow up you are the one who builds life, you build it, hey! ... I'm sorry that when you were a child you had people around you who did not know how to think, but now that you read this you have by "hobligation" with "h" leave that at once.

Remember that you are the one who allowed all those things about stuttering, now you think what you think because you interpreted everything that people said and created a concept of stuttering. If you now think that stuttering is the most horrible thing that could have happened to you, reflect that deep down that idea was put together by others, you took a bit of here, of this, of that and now you have a mega-concept of what it is: REALLY STUNNING .... and? And? -------- And? ----------> and the house without sweeping. Have you ever wondered if someone can go to the bathroom for you? Can you see a match in the eyes of others? When do you die, do you die with all your relatives or do they bury only you? Are you born with another person inside? Who is the one who thinks things out? At this moment you think that I am the one who tells you this, it is not like that, your mind makes as if what you are reading is me who is telling you, your mind plays with you, you are the one who reads, interprets and at this moment The one who draws the conclusions from what you are interpreting, I am just a mere idea that you have of me, but me? You don't know me, you don't know what I think, or how I don't think, or what ideas I have, you don't know anything about me, what you know about me is an idea of you when you read me, but I, my dear friend, am only your mind, the other is an invention of yours. That is why realizing how you live is the main step for change, you do not live at the pantry of others, you are not the result of multiplication, you are multiplication, Hey! Make no mistake baby, feet on the ground, you are the one who lives this life, everything that has happened in your life and what will happen is your responsibility, because in the end what happens outside has to be interpreted by you and you are the one who draws the conclusions. That is why what you can think of me says more about you than about me, because you are the one who thinks so ... °°°° epaaa °°°° ... attentive to the fact that the hurricane is coming very soon, well ... believe that the people have been the culprit of your stuttering, fate, life, God, etc ... puts you in a position where you can not even control, how can you control from below? If you want to know where the exit is, you will have to climb the mountain to see it, from the top you can fly. If you saw the number of people who constantly excuse themselves from hell who live for someone, that is very silly, I really understand that there are really stupid people to teach, say things, raise, whatever, but you can't ask for much of them either ... Imagine that the culprit for your stuttering was the teacher you had at school because he always scolded you when you stuttered and from there your stuttering increased, that you can ask that person if that person did not really know what he was doing, you cannot ask him to a salt shaker than salt when it doesn't give more salt! For this reason, to finish this topic, I would like you to reflect a lot on those who have blamed your stuttering, because later you will realize that it was your movie, people try to be what they are, to live their own human experience , there are few reasons to really accuse someone, even life itself, if that were the case, it would not be worth staying in that either, it is very sad when many boys stay in the pool of tears for events that have already happened, hey you can no longer do nothing, life has no reverse for now, the important thing is there is this "X", what can I do with this "X", my reason is that this "X" can make a big "Y". It starts with what there is, with what there is. Look, the oldest are not the ones who have everything to start with, but from what little they have they make it big, that's the difference, because sometimes when you have everything to start you don't even start… because you will always think that something is missing…. (excuses, everything that follows from then on are excuses, someone used to say that when someone makes excuses it always looks good, that's why people do it, obviously it's a feeling, then it breaks your soul)

The Ego

The Egoooo yes yes yes yes yes, This word is I think one of the most rejected or misused in culture, when someone tells you that you have an ego, people use it for the wrong, but in my opinion, this is already very subjective, the ego is what will make you a mountain in the middle of the landscape. The ego is what comes out of your veins that others can notice, but in real terms the ego is that little inner voice that tells you everything at all times, it is the mind that speaks to you in order to say it in some way, my great teacher Luismo Describe as the pixie, the one that tells you that it is right or that it is wrong or judges every situation whether it is for your good or for your evil, be careful with that, for your evil? Well, yes, the ego does not determine what will be good for you, it simply acts on what you have sown in your thoughts.

At this moment when you read this there is an internal voice that tells you things, she always talks to you, this is good, I think so, mmmm maybe, will it? I don't know, I have doubts. When you are in a conference and you listen to the announcer, the ego tells you: it's okay, I don't believe it, when will I get out of here? That same ego is the one that appears when you are the one who speaks in public: others are looking at me, what a shame, what a scare, ahiii noo what will they think of me? I will be able to do it? ...etc etc...

The Ego has been greatly crushed by the truth, many say that you should not get carried away by the ego, because that will always keep you in the comfort zone, the ego does not want you to progress, it takes care of you, it rejoices you, in my Different opinion from many others is that: The ego is the best there is. My ego is in the clouds because I have cultivated it, I have sown thoughts of value in it, it does not control me, the ego is a result of my thoughts, as I have taught my ego to always grow and risk at all times. He tells me that I can give more, that I can launch myself, that I deserve it, that I am the best, that I am worth a lot like this… .this is my ego. What is your ego?

The ego is nothing more than the sum of thoughts that you have cultivated throughout your life, although it can control you or you can control it, nothing more, understanding the ego is something that takes time because you believe that everything that it It tells you it is true, but there comes a point where you have to see what triggers the ego, what food you give the ego so that it thinks in such a way, so that in situations like being in a group of people it tells you: uiiiii look at how he laughs at you, what a shame…. Or be careful they may notice that you stutter… things like that….

There is a phrase that says: Realize the thinker of the thought. It is not the thought that you will have to see, because this is a result of what you cultivate, you will have to see the thinker of the thought, that is, the one who sows the thoughts, in a few words it is you, but not you superficially, it is you in Deep in your heart, I know it sounds a bit Hollywood, but you will have to peel off the onion skins to find the center that determines why the ego tells you such things.

Identifying if an ego is good or bad is easy, it is just to think if you have done something interesting in your life or have become stagnant, this you will have to see in every way because the ego changes depending on the situation, for example if you are very good at drawing, deep down you know you're good, you've practiced it, you've seen it, the ego will tell you things like: —Wow, you're a crack, I draw better than many— when it comes to drawing a group drawing, the ego He will tell you: —You will do it better than anyone else, you are brilliant at this— and deep down you feel good. But if in the case of stuttering you have an ego on the floor and you know that others are above you, if you have low self-esteem, if you give priority to others, if you feel that stuttering is bad, the ego will do is to tell you things like: —Don't talk, wait for someone else to speak, what a pity they will think when they speak, I won't talk about this because it doesn't go with the topic, I don't know whether to say something, uiiii I stuttered a bit I bear—… ..etc… etc … etc … in that case the ego in stuttering situations has to be put up again (this is very common for people who tell me that they have high self-esteem because they are good at the other, and I tell them : "Would you like someone to be generous only with strange people or with everyone? Would you like them to be honest with you only on some occasions or in everything? - That is the same thing that happens with the ego, how much you feed your ego well , this does not become something that determines the situations, the ego simply becomes you.

Nor do I want to understand myself as if I were talking about the ego in the form of self-centeredness, that's different, what's more, self-centeredness is when someone believes himself more than others and shows it, a person with a high ego does not need those blowjobs, he is already tall You do not need to demonstrate anything, or make others feel low, a person with a trained ego makes others get the best, there is the difference between being egocentric and having a high ego.

There are a photo that I really like that became very popular. The photo shows how the dogs compete in speed with a cheetah (cheetah) and the cheetah stays in place, the dogs therefore run like crazy. At the end of the photo it appears: when you grow up you don't need to prove anything.

The Arguments in Overcoming

To give you a quick review, the arguments are thoughts that must be created to establish new beliefs, which concludes that we have to make the beliefs you have now start to falter by creating new thoughts as opposed to what you think.

When people go to the psychologist they don't really expect what the psychologist tells them, people expect them to agree with them, or for the psychologist to say something that has to do with what the person tells them.

Most of the time it does not work like that, people go to the psychologist and he gives them a totally different perspective, a perspective that clashes with what they are thinking, and that is where the real key to change is, you see! The key to change is that many times what you are going to read you will not like, you will be against it, you will not find sense of it, that is normal, but believe me it is the key to change.

Can you imagine someone going to the psychologist and saying: "I'm really bad, my partner has left me, my family is gone" and the psychologist says: OHH by God! Yes, that is bad, that is horrible, how could your partner have left you? It can't be! (Please !!) Do you think that would help for anything? I would give the person the reason to feel comfortable that's it. Many things that I will tell you are going to bother you and understand that it has to be that way. I constantly tell people that if something has bothered them or they have doubts, it is there, when something scares you, if you continue there you will realize that the fear was a ghost that you had created.

What we will see from here next is a stream of content that you may have heard, seen, do not believe, doubts, etc ... etc ... Anyway, they are things that you have not consciously applied, it has simply been something anecdotal , something you ever heard that entered one ear and left the other. In this case it is different, because first I tell you that I have already been good years in this matter, second, because I have treated thousands and thousands of people, third, because the path that people follow with me or without me to overcome and correct stuttering goes through this same path, there is no other way, hopefully, there may also be, throughout my life I do not know it, perhaps ... in any case this is the way not only to overcome stuttering but to transform your life.

I warn you that when you start reading, continue until you finish the book, do not judge by just getting to the beginning of a book, many people leave things halfway being one of the main problems in society today, people live in a kind of multitasking (Multitasking? What the heck is that blow job?) As it was said in the back, that leaving things half done or picking here and picking there is a blowjob... do you know why some people never find a way? It is not because they do not find it, yes, there are literally many (in stuttering there are many paths that do not lead to anything the truth, but let's say that is not the problem) it is because they never finish one. Keep in mind that not finishing things like this book leads to this becoming routine in your life, it becomes a vice, again: the most important thing is that you keep in mind the word: PROCESS.

PROCESS ------> Tattoo it on your mind very big !!

Welcome to the World of Overcoming Stuttering.

Thanks for being here. Always GREAT

The Overcoming Mindset

For everything in this life the mental part is needed, a successful man does not come from nothing to success, it can happen in some cases, but most have a mentality of success, it is that oriental reflection that says: if you want to hunt the servant you will have than to become the servant.

There is a certain structure that makes up the mentality in this case the Overcoming and there are 4 key elements that we are going to take into account. You have to know that the human being is practically composed of these 4 things, when you have all these 4 things aligned your life practically goes like the clouds.

The first is the thoughts (you will tell me at this moment: ahiii again with the thoughts) yes! thoughts, there is nothing to say after all we have talked about this, later we will touch on this more in depth.

The second thing is the words: the words are blown away by the wind, have you heard that phrase or when someone says, from the saying to the fact there is a long way (hahahaha the phrase is higher, I know) the truth is that the words can go Like the clouds, in your mind they are piercing like holes, each word that comes out of your mouth will be sending a small signal to your mind making it stronger, imagine that the words although they do not have enough weight immediately, in the long term they are a cannon . I do not know if you have seen when the doors or the wood are attacked by termites, the truth is when this happens, the door is still normal, you see some small balls on the ground that are insignificant, days and weeks go by and everything is the same, the door is completely intact, a few months go by and when you open the door it falls off, when you grab the wood it breaks, this is how words act.

The third and not because it is the third is less important, but in my opinion it is the most important, when before I thought that thoughts were everything, the truth is that feelings are what makes your process grow exponentially (when I'm talking about exponential growth, I mean multiplied growth, you can make the process meet the normal times, but if you want to make the stuttering process like rockets you will have to give more value to feelings) in my personal story I I thought that thoughts were what made a person change, then I realized that the feeling that has to do with emotions is what really facilitates change undoubtedly (it is not coherent when someone thinks something and feels something, think what anyone can think, feel takes a much more detailed process)

The fourth is the actions (for the mentality such as overcoming there are actions that must be carried out obviously, not everything falls from the sky) when we talk about actions we talk about doing, starting, it is like when you say: I am going to sing and you stay Sitting there, when someone says I'm going to count, he starts practicing, reading songs, balancing his voice, rehearsing, humming music, toning the treble, bass, etc. get to: to get to do. I understand that there may be a confusion between the actions and the facts, let me clarify it for you once: it is the same.

These 4 elements that I mentioned are the main ones in the process of overcoming stuttering, the idea is to be able to align these four elements in such a way that your life focuses in that direction, the greatest point you can reach is to say words constructive, to think positively, to feel enjoying yourself and to take actions to improve your life.

The Thoughts

Again the thoughts, yeah! Again hahahaha…. You have to understand that thoughts deserve a throne in the process of overcoming knowing that feelings control life of course, but I really like thoughts because we constantly think about things, interpret and are drawing conclusions. To understand that what you think now will be practically what you will think tomorrow is to understand the logic of thoughts, to understand that what you think tomorrow will be what you will think in a week, two weeks and the next month is to understand the logic of thoughts.

As it was said before, thoughts are cultivated, they are created. How? ----> Daily ---- the answer remember is: PROCESS. We are beings of customs as well as habits, we get up in the morning and we have the habit (many) of looking at the cell phone, when before we looked at the window, now we look at the cell phone, we have the habit of having breakfast daily (being able to skip breakfast, many prefer to have breakfast) some have the habit of saying hello, others do not, etc ... etc.

What I mean by this is that we are beings who have customs for society, which we are establishing in our lives, then each one takes different habits that we usually repeat daily. Here it is important to begin to realize that thinking becomes habit. We are going to put the case of when you meet someone who interested you, those interests that you saw you start to transform into thoughts, you get up and there are certain moments where those memories of that person come to you, and that's how you think about them every day, until you The mind begins to create an image of that person of whom you have created, that image you were cultivating with the first thoughts, and thus little by little you fall in love through the thoughts.

In the case of stuttering it is the same, imagine that you think that having stuttering is a problem and that it is best to hide it. Every day when you talk to people you will think that it is best to hide your stuttering, when you meet your friends, family members you will try as much as possible to think that you cannot stutter, that it would not be good for them to realize (obvious people already know, but your mind is very playful) days, weeks, months go by and you create the thought of hiding the stuttering by what they will say. * You can tell that you have created that thought if somewhere they touch on the subject of stuttering and you already want the earth to swallow you *

Every day is a day to build new thoughts that give you mental strength, you will have to do it daily, every day, the thoughts are constant, so you must be very careful and take a step before thinking about it (we will handle this later) what I anticipate is basically a record of creating constructive thoughts that break the old paradigms.

Words

Words as well said up there is what we speak, what we often say to ourselves, or what we say to others, look at one thing, I want you to keep this in mind: Never play with words, because The end ends up being fulfilled, the words have power, if you are going to use them take advantage of them, remember that life has its double meaning, if you try to play saying things that are not at the end the omelette always goes around.

I will tell you a story that a friend of mine told me: At that time my friend was with his partner, they were very focused on their future plans, they did not think about children for the moment; But something happened that completely changed their lives, one day my friend tells me that he meets a kind of man who knew mystical things (he told me this way) my friend told me that the man handled some very curious words, that when She saw him and said: "Congratulations, your wife is going to have a baby girl." He stared at the man thinking What the hell? a girl? We haven't thought about that, my friend said. The man only said to him: "Okay." Later my friend would find out that his partner was pregnant.

In this story we can conclude two things: either the guy was a crack bastard or he really knew how to handle words, my friend tells me that those words stuck to him like daggers, and that is that the words when you say them can have so much power that even the other ends up turning that into reality.

There is another story that a boy told me about his friend who, being with her partner, became pregnant, she did not want to have the baby, although she did not want to abort it, she was in a dilemma, although all this was invaluable for her, which she was terrified of telling her father that she was pregnant. She was so afraid that people would find out about her that she decided not to comment on anything. When people

65

asked her about what happened to her partner, she said that she was not pregnant, everyone who asked her if she had taken care of herself, or if she was pregnant, denied it. When the pregnancy symptoms began, she told people that she was only a little sick, that she was not pregnant, the curious thing about this story happens that after several months her belly had no change, her father, although he noticed it strange, she did not perform no change in your tummy. She arrived one day where she could not support that lie, she told her father that she was pregnant, after telling her this, after a few days her belly swelled up, having her baby a few weeks (a story very curious the truth)

It is said that Rocky Marciano was the best boxing fighter in the world, known as the Legend, the champion of champions, it is said that the Rocky Balboa movie is inspired by this man. This boxer won all his fights considered the top man in time, having to his credit 49 victories in 49 matches, that is, the guy won everything, and to be scared with the figures: 43 fights were by Knockout, a machine Actually, the most curious fact about Rocky Marciano is that before going into the ring he always said: I am the best, I am the champion! I'm the best! I am the champion! This was repeated several times, it was even said that many times he told his opponent to intimidate him, to make it clear to him who the champion was (a story that shows the mental power that words have)

Of course, it is good to differentiate between words and thoughts, although it is clear to understand that words are often the result of what we think, although this is not entirely true. You know, many people, if not most, end up saying things that they do not think, many times out of fear of what they will say or simply because they are out of focus (when I speak of blur in this case I mean that the thoughts go one way and the words for another)

Once I was doing an English course I spoke with a colleague named Ismael, this was a boy with a great personality, incredible, he spoke wonderful things, what surprised me the most was his mentality, he seemed made of steel, a guy that you you saw and everything was going like fireworks, but Ismael was always short, so much money, people, friends, something, I don't know ... it was as if he was short of breath ... but all this would pass when you talked to him. Once I remember that we had a class where we had to move a lot, do dynamics and we ended up exhausted on the floor very tired, I remember that we began to speak as we used to, but this time within a different context because we were in a moment of relaxation, exhausted but quiet. Suddenly Ismael spoke very strange, he said words that had never come out of his mouth, I remember him saying that he was a boy without luck, that he was scared of everything, that he was very shy, that he considered himself very poor and felt very lonely. There I understood that Ismael c he began to speak from his heart, there I understood that the real Ismael was speaking. I remember this story a lot, you know ... because I drew a conclusion that day: it is not that words are not important, only that when your mind thinks things, your heart another and your words another, you are out of focus. As much as you can speak the bible if in your mind you do not have a strong mentality what you speak will be like the air, only people will believe it, but inside you will know the ordeal that you live. Look, many guys lied to me several times with stuttering, because when you start the process you have to tell your own story, in this case they told it to me, the truth is that I realized that they were lying to me when they told me things like: "stuttering in my life is not a problem, I just don't like having it" "the truth is, I surround myself with people, sometimes I feel uncomfortable, but it's not that I'm afraid of exposing my stuttering" I pay so much attention to stuttering, I already live with that. on the letter p, I get stuck, it's just that, the rest I handle well " After all these sentences I realized that behind his words there were cobwebs that covered his thoughts, you have seen how people are not able to see their own spike, it is easy to see the mistakes of others, the most difficult thing is to see one itself, that is really the mastery of life. A great philosopher said that the hardest work is work with oneself (literal)

Affirmations

The Affirmations !! Affirmations are not a special topic, truth or a concept that you have to learn from, affirmations arc a tool that will help you in the process of overcoming stuttering. Whether affirmations can help you or not is up to you.

I do tell you that there are millions of cases worldwide where affirmations have helped people, in my case, wow! too! because in addition to the fact that you are listening to them every day, writing, internalizing they are like blows that hammer your brain, remember the phrase that says: "water does not pierce the rock because of its hardness but because of its constancy"

You have to understand that repeating certain words like a parrot is useless, nor would I like to say that it does not work, something ends up affecting you but it does not have much weight, it is minimal (I remember a lot when I once heard a truthful fact that says: people Those who commit suicide do not commit suicide because one day they decided to take their own lives, it is something that is woven with a little seed, one day those people crossed a little thought of wanting to leave and every day that idea became bigger, What's more, even from joke to joke, ideas are believed, that is why the brain does not measure jokes, he does not know what that is)

Likewise, repeating itself has no weight from my point of view, in any case the affirmations as such have "NOTHING TO DO WITH THAT" repeating does not make any sense, just as it enters it leaves, a typical phrase that says: it enters through one ear and it comes out the other. (As I said before: something may fit you, but why do things that do not have so much weight, is for example when you think of a tool to disassemble a computer, do you prefer a nail or a screwdriver?)

Affirmations are powerful phrases that reflect who you want to be. Affirmations inspire you, motivate you and recharge you with energy to believe that idea that you are expressing in your mind, a universal law says: repeat an idea many times and you will end up believing it.

I'm sorry if I go around the same thing a lot, but I have to first make things clear about the affirmations, the idea of the affirmations is that you do them daily, every day, however, take care that by doing it daily it does not become something automatic, but that you focus on the affirmations. Affirmations as I said above are powerful phrases, they are made in the present and are made up of constructive insight.

For example: a powerful statement is: "I feel calm when I am talking to my friends at the university, when I talk to them they all admire me, I feel like the king of the conversation since I am worth too much, people really want to be with me"
This statement that you saw earlier is made up of the present, that is, it is in NOW mode, it does not say: I would "feel" calm with my friends ... nor does it say: When I "spoke" everyone admired me ... nor in Generic way: when you "talk" with friends you have to "feel" calm ... that kind of affirmations do not work, they do not talk about now, they do not vibrate towards you, they do not say anything, they remain in the air.

It is also normal that when you hear these types of statements you do not vibrate with them because you do not believe them, it is normal not to believe them for now, maybe they sound strange to you, or like lies that you are telling yourself, maybe you feel that they are masks or what Whatever, that doesn't matter, nobody has started to believe in something by believing, belief is built, my friend, as well as trust, the mind, everything in this life is a process. In the end, you will take those ideas like coffee. Your mind will always try to pull you where you are going, the idea is that you pull where you want to go, that is the power of affirmations.

Something important is to try as much as possible that all the statements have the "I am" note that the word "I am" has such a powerful connotation that when someone says: "I am" it really is, hahahaha, it's funny but it is Really, you have surely heard people say: it is that I am not good for that, and it is true, not only because they tell him but he knows very well that it is so and that is why he reveals it with that statement: "I am"

I remember once my great friend Caio told me not to say: —I am a stutterer— but rather: —I am a stutterer— because when you say I am a stutterer you are defining yourself at the level of being, in a few words you are making your life is completely defined by stuttering, the I am is global, stuttering is an annex of your life, it does not mean that when you say I am it is wrong, not at all, it is acceptable, indeed, it can give you a greater degree of responsibility , and that's good, but the reality is that you have stuttering and at the same time you have fluency, sometimes you access one and other times you access the other, because behind stuttering is the being that is you, no there is nothing that defines you behind being, that is why having stuttering makes you able to see it, manage it, have it in hands.

Note: that above is very relative, no matter how you say it, the important thing is that in none of the statements you feel pain, rejection or something that has to do with suppressing stuttering.

"Having is different from rejecting" when I have something I look at it, that does not define me, I have achieved it that is why I decide to take hands on the matter (in any case, this part as I said is for you to take it sportingly)

The I am is the most powerful beginning to define you, that is why people say: I am an artist, I am a musician, I am bad, I am generous. What I really want to get to is that you understand that the words that make up the affirmations have a value.

There are other types of affirmations that are words that although they are important do not have as much weight as a powerful affirmative phrase based on a real context. What the hell do I mean by all that stuff?

Look at this statement: "When I have to exhibit at school, Mauricio Hernández, I do it safely. I feel so empowered! I AM a God in what I

70

say, I dominate them all, people applaud me because they know that I AM the best speaker in the school. When I'm there in front, everyone looks at me, smiles and I feel like I don't give a damn what they think, even if they like me first, always me and definitely me, I am a complete being, what matters most to me is what I always say Wow! I am someone incredible "

This statement above is from a boy who stuttered a lot when exhibiting at school and we handle these types of statements. That statement has a place: school. A concrete situation: present in class. A context: expose with colleagues. A time that is: present.

A statement like: "I am powerful" does not have as much weight, it may have it if you feel that you vibrate in it or it gives you strength just listening to it, it can be clear, but in my experience with people the best affirmations are the affirmations that They are made in the present tense, they have a specific context, they are focused on a goal and they determine a specific place.

The ideal would be for you to see what are the everyday situations you have and try to reconstruct them to how you would like them to be, that is the best way to make a statement, remember that statements have to be in the present, the idea that they are in the present It is not because it sounds more beautiful, it is because it becomes credible, it is not something that will happen or happened, it is something that you feel it NOW, that is like saying I - "I will believe" that I can cross the bridge - it is ridiculous that - I "will have faith "that I do well in the exam nooo hahaha! I have faith that I am doing well on the exam.

See what is a curious anecdote with cigarette labels. Before the labels of cigarettes (cigars) they said: smoking can kill, smoking can give cancer ... after a while they saw that those labels did not work very well, people continued to consume tobacco, so they decided to put: smoking causes cancer, smoking causes lung damage, etc ... with this better results were evidenced, even so they saw that the best way was to put it in "PRESENT" and "PERSONAL": Smoking kills you, smoking gives you cancer, smoking damages your lungs etc ... what do you think ah? Curious no?

Another mistake that many people make is putting negative words with a positive context, as I told you above, the brain does not determine if something is good or bad, it just takes the thought as such and keeps it. For example: "I am not a shy person" here the intention is to be safe, but it is a wrong statement, what will your brain think when it sees this? "In shyness" Imagine that you want to stop eating croissant and all day you repeat yourself: —I don't want to eat Croissant - I don't want to eat Croissat - I don't want to eat Croisant - What will the brain think? In croissant of course !! So to conclude this part you have to make the affirmations using affirmative words with a positive vibe, not like these phrases:

I am someone who does not think small
I speak well to others, although sometimes I feel sorry
I am not afraid because I am powerful
Some situations make me nervous, but I know I have to move on
I am not someone who rejects stuttering
I don't care about the approval of others
What others say does not interest me because I am not someone who pays attention to that
I do not hide from people

Finishing the book I leave you some affirmations so that you have as guides, many of these affirmations I handled them with many people.

Note: something that I do have to tell you is that there is nothing more powerful than you to make the affirmations, because you are the one who knows the reality of what you live, where you move, what are the situations where you feel bad, etc ... That is why I repeat: Overcoming and correcting stuttering is an "INDIVIDUAL" process.

I started the affirmations since I began my improvement until today that I still do, it is a vitamin for me, it gives me strength, courage! The most important thing is that when you listen to the affirmations, do it constantly and internalize each one of them as if you were there.

What I used to do was write the affirmations in a notebook every day, I also recorded all the affirmations with my own voice and I put some background music to make them more inspiring, the idea of the affirmations is that they have an inspiring approach.

Note: A lot of guys used to record the affirmations to me as if they were reading, that is very silly, record them as if you were going to compete in a race, as if you were encouraging yourself to live, skinny! You have to put fire in this life, how can you inspire yourself by recording some affirmations by reading? noooo, do them with passion, imagine that you are climbing a hill and you only have one section to go, if you do not arrive, you fall and you die, you need to save yourself and you are there to say a few words of encouragement: what would you say to yourself?

There is something that happened but I want you to understand it, the word "how it is said" is more important than the word: "what is said" many will say that the message is the important thing, but for sure it was proven that the "form" In saying things is more important than the message, people grasp the way of saying things more, because in our evolution we begin to communicate with gestures, with tones, with sounds. The words, the alphabet as well as the language of came later. It's different when I tell you: —Hey, you look good— with a body shape and gesture that I don't care, would you feel it? but if I tell you: hey you look good !!! in a surprised and admired way, denoting surprise, there if you would feel more right?

So remember that when you do affirmations, do them with energy, that same energy is what you will hear every day. As I just revealed to you, I wrote affirmations, recorded them and then listened to the affirmations every day at any time that I could; it is so much that when I was alone I recited them out loud and I felt powerful. Ask yourself something: people usually listen to things that do not contribute to them, why don't you start listening to things that contribute to you and that also motivate you? You have to be very creative, creativity is not obtained, it is sought with strategies, it looks for all the situations where you can do something different and you will find the results you are looking for.

The Visualizations

Visualization is another of the tools to promote overcoming stuttering. Not to be confused with vision, they sound similar, but it is different, although both have to do with visualizing a landscape or a reality in the present, the two are completely different.

Tangle-free visualizations is the day-to-day of how you would like things to be. For example: my situation at work is that I get to the office, I have to say hello to the boss, I stutter a lot, then I have to meet with colleagues, I feel uncomfortable, then I have to call many people and I have a terrible time, etc ... etc .. That situation, which is a situation of stress, discomfort, panic, call it whatever you want, you have to reinvent it again by visualizing it in such a way that it goes in coherence to where you want to go.

You are at a point "A" with a reality and you will reach a point ------------ ----------------> "B"

To get to that point B, which is where you want to go, which is the vision, you will have to make small visualizations that are aimed at that vision.

So the correct visualization would be: I wake up in the morning and meditate about how my day is going to be: "I arrive at the office, I see and feel like I greet the boss with enthusiasm, I see myself flowing like never before and if I stutter I feel like I am I pass it through the eggs, then I meet with my colleagues and share a short joke which everyone laughs, or I start to make jokes, I see how I feel good, I am in the clouds, then I see myself calling many people with some desire and a passion to speak, I see myself there advising people, taking command, having control, if someone does not go with that I see myself sending him for a fly "

The visualizations are linked to the affirmations, every day you have to make affirmations like every day in every moment you have to make visualizations, not only in the morning. Surely you have ever heard about the power of visualization, I don't want to go into energetic or esoteric things or ancestral energies, none of that, what happens with visualizations in scientific terms is focus, visualizations become real because you make your mind focuses on what you really want so actions, words, gestures, everything is accommodated to what your mind visualizes every day.

When I started to overcome stuttering I visualized a lot, especially speaking in public, for me this visualization was complex because I was very scared, I felt my hands sweat just thinking about it, time passed and that visualization felt more normal, As a daily routine, I no longer generated those bodily things, what's more, situations were presented to me to be able to carry out those visualizations, it was as if the world adjusted to what I was thinking, then everything settled down and the visualizations always materialized, it was like magic, but it wasn't magic, my mind vibrated in that visualization.

There is something that is very interesting and that is scientific and that is that when people draw, if they draw their goals, objectives or what they want about things that they have been afraid to do in life out of fear, or because of what they think, or because of There is a lack of money, for whatever reason, when people draw that, it has been proven that the emotional charges they had from not being able to carry it out go down; what they draw becomes more accessible, it can be felt, it feels more tangible.

The Emotions

Ayaaa yaaaiiii !!! We arrived where the maximum point of the TOP-TOP-TOP is. This without any doubt is the most discredited concept of humanity using words like: rationality, logic, coldness, without mind, without emotion.

Beforehand I tell you that emotions are what you will end up enjoying the most, although especially mmm I'm thinking the truth a lot about how to explain emotions to you ... You have to understand that emotions or feelings are the trigger for an event, for example: when someone tells you It says that you are useless, your emotions may shrink, you feel pain deep down, that pain is a reaction that has arisen from that event.

To understand the type of emotion that results when something happens to you is to know yourself very deeply. People who do very well in life usually know their emotions a lot, they are masters of this, because when you know your emotions you know your advantages as well as disadvantages, knowing this you have control of starting to improve some aspect of your life more. easily.

Someone who does not know their emotions is also very easy to manipulate, because when they say something to them that person will say "yes immediately", without asking themselves, do I like this, what will I do? Deep down, he knows that it doesn't go with his emotions, but even so, he continues, then that is where the frustration arrives, why it always comes back to the same thing. If we could define the process of stuttering, we could say that it is divided into two: those who pass the process despite the turns, or those who stay spinning; those who stay around are people who do not want to see or leave there always arriving: THE SAME.

Let's put a context of the typical common stuttering: You are talking to a person, that person begins to bombard you with questions in a row, as you are not used to being bombarded with questions you begin to "feel" uncomfortable since you "feel" that you cannot handle these kinds of situations. From now on you start to sweat, you stutter more and your answers are short, blocked, what you want most is for that situation to end. In those moments you may be thinking: "It happened again, aahh this situation again, how will I be staying in front of that person." Here you also "feel" how your self-esteem is on the ground, you understand that it is a situation that repeats itself, but deep down you don't like those situations, after the conversation is over you stay there saying: —give me dirt—. What happens next is that your emotions play against you, you feel like you were worth nothing in that conversation, frustration of how you stood before those people, you may feel more bad if it was a relative. The typical as the most common is that you feel that you stuttered a lot and that is something that makes you feel bad because you "think" that you control stuttering and you have it more or less balanced at such a point, when you already raise that rod a lot, then already there you do not like. The biggest frustration someone has with stuttering is three: that he stuttered again, that he stutters a lot, or that he can't stop stuttering; Of those three things is where your feelings party.

When you do not know your feelings is when you let them show in each presentation, it is not because your feelings are bad, nor when I mean that they play with you is something bad, nahhh at all, they are part of you, it is the game that you created them, later we will see something commonly called the ego, at this moment remember that what your feelings do is your responsibility.

Why are emotions the most important thing or is it what you will end up changing? Because these logically determine how you feel. We human beings are emotional beings, every decision we make is made from the emotions, although here you will tell me: —I have made many decisions leaving aside the emotions—, I will answer you: that is a great blowjob, you stop On one side the emotions because deep down the emotion of feeling that you are letting yourself be carried away by it is greater. In short, when someone makes a decision, for example, to continue in school even if they do not like it, they really do not continue because they do not like it, their emotion at what their parents may think or feeling that they have no education can more than the feeling not to like it.

Remember that scientifically speaking we are emotional beings and therefore emotions have the greatest weight in overcoming stuttering. Emotions as well as thoughts are created since childhood, you cultivate them, you feed them and it becomes automatic. If such a situation happens, I react in such a way, that same reaction is repeated whenever that situation happens, in a nutshell, emotions become a habit. If we put a real example it would be: When a person feels fear when speaking in public, that feeling will always be perpetuated and will continue-will continue until the same person has to see That feeling hurts your growth in life, why? because it makes no sense to be afraid in that situation, we will see this later.

The key to changing emotions is to realize, (at this moment I want to clarify something for you so that you do not think something different: most of what we are going to talk about is the same, it is the same repeated in many different ways, you have to know that the principles will always remain principles, then the topics that we will deal with you will see that it returns to the same thing again, because everything is intertwined, this is like a network, everything revolves around the same) I open again (that is normal, so that everything is very clear you will have to have everything very clear, remember that everything has to do with everything)

After realizing, you have to start something known as emotion management, the word management is something that can generate misunderstandings since the truth is that you do not manage anything, or you feel what you feel or you stop feeling it. What is going to be done is a feeding of constructive emotions, there are emotions that give you that freshness, make you feel good, give you confidence, for example: the emotion when something you have always wanted happens, the emotion of realizing that People love you, the emotion of seeing someone, the feeling it gives you when you do something that you like, all these are emotions that you have to keep in mind in order to build them and that they have a greater weight.

Although evolutionarily we develop with the most pessimistic emotions, now the world has changed, it is normal that negative emotions carry more weight because before in history, if we were not alert or we painted everything beautifully, an animal would eat us, imagine being in the jungle Feeling that the landscape is wonderful, you would be an easy target, that's why we develop that alertness, that negativity to resolve situations in flight or attack.

In the case of stuttering, most people have negative feelings against it, although it is not the stuttering that generates those feelings, it is the interpretations you make of stuttering that triggers those feelings, remember that everything is what you least think it is . Stuttering is not the main problem, it is all that you generate around it that makes you live a life like this: either a shitty life or a happy life, there are no half parts here.

When people think about stuttering, we already know what they think, that triggers several feelings that are distributed in different situations: Being with family members generates certain feelings, being with strangers also generates certain feelings, when you speak, the way you speak, When you are alone and you talk, it generates certain feelings in you, when you speak in front of an audience, when you go to buy something, when you make a call, when they call you, when you read, when you reflect on your life and think about stuttering it generates feelings, in All this you have to be attentive to observe, which is what you feel in each situation, from there you have to begin to knock down those false feelings. You have to --- obligatorily --- with "h" release those feelings, obviously you will not release them, it is impossible, you will have to change them. Have you ever heard that letting go of a habit is almost impossible, because it is the same with emotions, I don't mean impossible because it sounds very blunt ... "It is very complex" ... it will cost you an egg to do so. The only thing you can do is replace them with new feelings, that way it will be simpler.

Do you remember that at the beginning I told you that feelings are what will end up transforming you, it is true, imagine that the above changes: when they call you you feel a joy because they call you, when you think to call someone you feel very secure, when you talk to family members You feel that you can contribute valuable things, when you talk to strangers you feel that you are someone with a high self-esteem who can always give the best, when you are thinking about your life with stuttering you feel that this can be the trigger to get where you want to go, when you go When you buy something you feel a lot of enjoyment when speaking, when you speak in public you feel that what others think of you does not matter to you, you feel so great that you can take that talk in your hands and be the leader of this, when you stutter You feel that you enjoy it, that you have a great time, you feel great every time you bring up the subject of stuttering.

Imagine all those feelings in those typical stuttering situations, it is a beast to think like that, you would be a (literal) monster who could say that that person cannot do what they want, please, you would be a God of your life, how someone Could you say that stuttering affects you if your thinking is on another level? that's why life is subjective, the perspective you have on something is your own perspective.

In conclusion, to close the subject of feelings you have to be very attentive, rather than attentive is to be: MMMMuyyyy detailed, very fine, the detail makes the difference, later on we will explain some Tips of what is the best way to realize what you think, feel and say.

The Acceptation

The acceptance, yes gentlemen: THE ACCEPTANCE. This word deserves a big prize worldwide, I think it is the word that defines happiness, Yes! That's how it is! If we could compare happiness with another word it would be with this one. Let me tell you with deep pride that this is the true path to "Overcoming" Stuttering (remember that overcoming is not correction, that goes for later, rabbit eye!)

Before entering into the matter with Acceptance I would like to make it clear = "That is not acceptance" because out there where you are there are many ideas of this that has nothing to do, the first thing is to understand that acceptance is not resignation, when someone he resigns himself, he has lost the courage to follow, he is exposed to what comes over him, when a person resigns it is because he is weak, weak, lacks character, trembles in the face of circumstances, he is someone who does not give 100 % in the life. When you give up it is because you have lost the will to live… .ehh shh quiet… .I understand that many with stuttering lose the motivation to live but that is exactly what can be lost the least, tell me how could you then reverse a situation if the desire is lacking, if the desire is missing you will lose all the games of life, the desire is what sustains you, the desire is what made you find a light in this book, you have to have that desire there, the least you can do is give their backs on life, those who turn their backs are those who surrender (remember that this society gives a lot of merit to people who surrender, because they show hurt, that's not bad, but you enter that vicious circle) I open again (that they feel sorry for you is very sad) I open (literal)

I'm going to give you a real typical example of the majority of stutterers with the concept of acceptance: Many of them reach a point where they say: —Hey that's it, I have a stutter, I can't do anything anymore and my life is horrible. Life shit on me, my parents are to blame, I have done everything, but nothing has come out to remove this stuttering— <----- -------- this is Resigning.

Acceptance is not giving up either, I understand that this attitude, although it is a little more than: I did the best I could, is certainly not an interesting attitude in stuttering. Pretend that stuttering loves it when you surrender to it because it happens to control you, or when you surrender to life you make it clean the dishes with you (I do not mean that giving up is bad in other aspects of life, for For example, when you know that something is not going to work, you give up with the idea of continuing with something else, or that you were an asshole to continue in something that does not give)

Acceptance is accepting situations as they are and taking a positive attitude towards this situation, accepting stuttering is to stop fighting with it, it is accepting that you have stuttering and that it is fine, that nothing happens ... absolutely nothing ... stuttering is with you for you, and if it is with you all your life then welcome, it may sound strange to you so far, but calm down, then you will understand, accepting stuttering makes you put yourself above it, because you do not have problem with this. When you have no problem with the problem, the problem is no longer a problem. The problems really, if you see them correctly, do not exist, it is just a label that you give to something that is above you, of course no one labels something thinking that it is above it, but if you saw that most do that (you don't think that is very silly, does it? Mmm so you can see that there are people who do it) if you determine that stuttering is a problem, disease, diagnosis, virus, whatever, let me tell you my friend that already before start you have lost the battle, what's more, close this book and put a candle to it.

Ask yourself something: Have you lived all this life struggling with stuttering? Have you been denying her? Cursing her? Saying things to him? Generating discomfort? ... a lot of things, do you think that following this same pattern you will change things? Obviously no, it is stupid to think that continuing like this will lead to a change, the changes are changes of thought, they are not thoughts of the now that you perpetuate.

The great teacher Buddha said that the key to happiness was detachment, we live a life full of attachments both material and mental, we become attached to love, family, people we know, comfort, a quiet life, the house, to everything ... that is normal ... we are human beings ... but understanding that attachment is something natural of the human being makes you understand reality, because when you know that being attached to something affects you, it is easier to let go of it, of course it hurts when we leave something but it liberates, nothing is more gratifying than feeling that you are liberated.

The same thing happens with stuttering and the perspective you have of it, you live attached to the idea that stuttering is a problem or is bad, that idea is useless, remember that what you resist the most persists, I will put it c are bold since this maxim is key when in the process you feel that you relapse into this. Stop tying the thoughts because in the end they are yours and to realize that the creative machine of these thoughts has a fault or is badly calibrated is to start looking for a new way of thinking.

Raising the idea of: it could be ... hey ... it could be that what you think is false -> it frees you, because you don't eat the story, neither the head of course, you don't eat anything, you start to determine what is more favorable for you. Adopting an attitude of acceptance with stuttering is the path to improvement.

Treat stuttering as if she were your best friend or friend, she has always been there for you, you created her, how could you reject something that you cultivated? Look ... the day you accept stuttering one hundred percent, totally, that day if stuttering has to go it will go away, if not it will be there with you, but you will see it differently, not as your enemy but as your best friend.

As a child they always took me to speech therapists, I remember once a woman was treating me who took several sessions with me. The truth was it was a bit frustrating since sometimes she had progress, other times not, well, she told me, until one day she told me something that I will always remember. I was sitting there in her office with my mother who accompanied me in the sessions and she said something that I have very much in mind:

I have a friend who stutters, he is very funny because when he speaks he makes us all laugh. "One day my friend told me that they were going to pop a balloon and they chose him to count 3,2,1 and pop the balloon, he told me that when he was at number" 1 "he said: uuuuu-uuunoo but already the balloon had burst and he was still finishing the count (laughs) so it was a lot of fun, my friend tells me that he likes to be like that, the truth is, I told him that it can be treated but he feels good about his stuttering "

The truth is that at that time she was very angry, when she told the story she thought: How can a guy like that feel good about stuttering? I imagined someone stupid, stupid, ugly, bored, feeling comfortable with stuttering, how was that possible? -The guy for me was an asshole, that day that person that I had never seen in my life made me small, small-

After this the speech therapist looked at my mother and me saying: there are people who feel good about their stuttering, —although from what I see you want to speak fluently and that is what we are going to work on—, I thought in my mind of course, Obviously I want to flow, that's what we're here for, right? Although I remember that I was little and was not so aware of things, I felt that something was wrong with me, if they took me there it was for something, to speak well I supposed, I believe that idea that I spoke badly so I wanted to speak well, not stutter , although he did not understand this "stuttering" very well either.

I always remembered that story, when I overcame stuttering I understood the story, because as a child I had not understood anything, if I had taken that path of the Lord I would have overcome stuttering long ago, because the true path was acceptance, man accepted himself as he was and brought out the best version of him.

When I accepted the stuttering, everything became so easy for me, the correction came alone, of course I had to go through a process that we will talk about later, but the mental part was so well structured that it became a piece of cake. The speech therapist without knowing had given me the answer, in the same way I later understood that she had no fucking idea what she was doing (that's normal, most speech therapists don't even know what they're doing, they haven't experienced this enough to help others, it is understandable and I do not judge them for that)

I did not see the answer, it is so much that I rejected that story, it seemed ridiculous, I was angry that she said that so silly, I thought of the man in that story as someone pathetic thinking that he could laugh at stuttering, if that was the worst thing that could happen to someone!

The path will always be that, my dear friend. Look ... what follows from here on is pure mentality, having this clear step is the key to overcoming. You may wonder how you do to accept stuttering if all your life you have been rejecting stuttering. Tell me how I do? We return to the same as before: if you want to change old thoughts you will have to create new thoughts.

One thing that many do that seems super natural to me is to repeat themselves like parrots who accept themselves, think that everything is going well, say nice things or other blowjobs. I understand from where they do it. Does all this really work? Mmm let me tell you that it is not that it does not work, it can work but that it is effective I do not think so, that it works mmmm little, it is more ... when you do what I will tell you, you will stop doing those other things that do not give you results, of course not you can let yourself be carried away by results, always let yourself be carried away by the: PROCESS

To conclude this topic: The most important Before overcoming is Acceptance, the true way to Overcoming as Correction is Acceptance. There is no one that I know who has overcome stuttering who has not gone through this path, it is rare that I find someone who says that they corrected or overcome stuttering by rejecting their stuttering, that is very rare you know (it can happen of course, this life It is a vineyard of many grapes, but it is very strange... I already tell you that I have been in this world of stuttering for a long time) The day you accept yourself totally, one hundred percent, completely, without a hint of rejection, stuttering will It will go if it has to go, if it does not go you will see it differently, remember that when you no longer have anything to lose is when the magic happens.

Has it ever happened to you that you already take something for granted but that you are still going on and things come out of one without so much roll, that is too common, when you say: there you know ... fuck it ... I'll do it ... if it works out okay and if not Also... .and it comes out... .and it comes out... .and you are like: ---- see ... what a curiosity ----- here few really start to think what happened. What happened was that since you are no longer attached to an idea that it turns out the way you want it to turn out, you don't care (I repeat: this is not synonymous with giving up or giving up, it is synonymous with letting flow, let whatever happens happen. , just change the perspective and you will see that what has to happen happens)

I will leave you one of my reflections that I learned in my overcoming, I keep it always present: When you change the way you see things, things begin to change. When you change the perspective of what happens this is transformed. Things always need an observer to be judged, the way you look at things makes life take that same position.

The Actions

Action as a concept seen above there is little to say at this point. This is practically the steps you will have to do to make everything you think, feel and say come true. There is a very curious aspect of religions, notice that most religions give a very high value to actions, because through actions, call them acts, facts, practices, more belief is given as importance to faith. There is a small fragment that is said a lot in the Catholic religion: —I have sinned in word, deed or mission. The word Work refers to actions, what I mean by this is that the value of actions is practically the result of aligning thoughts, feelings and words, what you will end up doing in the process of stuttering are actions that never before You thought you were going to enjoy yourself, those actions will be perpetuated making your life always align with that way of thinking.

I do not want to confuse the truth a lot, my motive is to be very honest with you and try to make you understand everything very well, that is why I repeat that there will be many topics that are touched several times, understand that it is the key for your mind to structure everything, everything is It is related to everything, it is not that the words are different from the thoughts or emotions or have to do with common situations, everything is related to everything, at the end of so much circling in the issues and giving those reviews it is very sure that you will have Everything super clear, with too high a clarity the ghosts that you had begin to disappear because you no longer believe the stories, you begin to be REALISTIC.

In each of the aspects mentioned above such as words, thoughts and emotions, you will have to put yourself in each of them to take actions that will replace the new paradigms. We will see this later, first of all stay with the idea that for anything an action is needed, if there is no action that supports it, I already tell you that you will return to the same thing, remember that beliefs are supported with ACTIONS.

The Self Steem

Another of the great elements that make up overcoming stuttering. Yes! Yes! Yes! The GREAT AND POWERFUL SELF-ESTEEM.

How many times have you heard people say that they have self-esteem on the floor, or others who say that that person has self-esteem through the roof (this is curious because people who have self-esteem on the floor speak of those who have it by the clouds thinking these are: very egocentric)

Sight. once and for all I will tell you the difference between someone egocentric and a person with self-esteem since many times they are confused. A person with self-esteem looks at himself, an egocentric person looks at others, a person with self-esteem values himself, an egocentric person values himself because he is afraid of being down before others, a person with self-esteem does not need the approval of others , a self-centered person constantly looks to others to feel superior.

So we could continue until we are tired ... but the idea is not to stay with this, the main idea is that you understand why self-esteem is one of the most valuable qualities in Overcoming.

It is necessary to be very clear with what we said before that this life is yours, for you, pretend that this life is a gift from you to you. The only one who is going to live this life is you, so the question that precedes it would be why the hell would you care about the opinion of others? I'm sorry if from now on I say rude, the truth makes me more practical when I want to say something without confusing the reader too much.

Self-esteem you have to know that it is built every day, a person with high self-esteem is difficult to fall into depression ... what's more ... it is rare for that to happen ... and if it did happen ... it would come out more easily than anyone. Something that if I have to tell you and hey I'm very sorry, but it is the reality, and it is that people with high self-esteem or who aim for this overcome stuttering faster than anyone else. There is another fact and I feel it again and it is that: the people who manage to have self-esteem through the roof that you could even say that that person if he had a clone would marry himself, are the people who surpass it by two by three, They rank the improvement, what's more, it is rare to see people who go through this with that type of personality (although personality mmmm not so much, this is rather something constructive)

Perooo ... there is something that maybe can encourage you and that surely you are in it and that is that most of the people who TODAY have high self-esteem were not before, the most extroverted people before were not, the most safe before they weren't. It is easier for a person to adopt security when it is not than for a person who is secure to stop being insecure and return to security, it is difficult when you are born with this ability to be able to sustain it, because you do not know in some way how you ended up there On the other hand, when you manage to achieve that self-esteem or security, you already know what the path has been and it is very rare that you fall back into low self-esteem.

We all know actor Tom Cruise from Mission Impossible, a guy who when interviewed has incredible empathy, communicates with the media, expresses himself super well, talks to everyone, the world of Hollywood says he is one of the actors with the best job, They also comment that she is a person who, when you talk to her, gives you her full attention. We see here then that this actor is a Hollywood superstar but ... do you think Tom Cruise was like that? The actor once commented in one of his interviews that he was the opposite, that both his personality, empathy and self-esteem had to be strongly developed since he considered himself a very scared person.

Many of the people you see with that high self-esteem were certainly not, it was something that out of necessity they had to acquire it, I really understand when someone does not want to have high self-esteem, I really understand it, but I have not met a person that he is happy with a low self-esteem, you see! I have had low self-esteem and high self-esteem, you can be happy or unhappy with low self-esteem or high self-esteem, but when I had low self-esteem I was never happy (I leave it to your discretion)

Nor should we confuse high self-esteem with being an extrovert, being an extrovert is a person who has more start, it is more of the patch, of the rubber, of surrounding himself, of people, but that does not mean that he has a high self-esteem. I have met many outgoing people who when you talk to them you realize that they are just a facade. There are many people with high self-esteem who do not need to greet everyone, be the life of the party, surround themselves with people, or things like that ... because security like self-esteem is something internal, it is carried within. That is why it is very curious when someone thinks that an extrovert has security or something like that, they can believe that it is seen, but inside they may be simmering.

I have cone I cid very quiet people, they say the basics, they are serious, they don't really smile much, they take things in a colder way and when you talk to them they have a security and self-esteem that you shit. The personality of each person is relative and that is why it is good to make these concepts clear, personality has nothing to do with low or high self-esteem, although I have to say that someone who is extroverted has a greater facility when it comes to building their self-esteem as well as when it comes to overcoming stuttering, but that does not mean that extroverts have self-esteem.

And now what the heck is Self-esteem? I understand that the above does not make it clear that it is self-esteem but makes it very clear that it is not. Knowing that it is not gives you a clearer idea of what self-esteem is. Self-esteem in a few words and to summarize what you can find out there that will be jets of things is: Having self-esteem is Valuing yourself completely = self-esteem is the same as loving yourself.

It sounds very stylish, we are all love, happiness, spirituality ... but it is the truth ... really, yes ... there is nothing else ... I wish I wasn't so sentimental at times explaining the more technical stuttering process, but that's the way it is. When someone loves themselves they really know that they are worth a lot, a special case is when you love someone, when this happens everything you see in that person is excellent, what's more, sometimes love is so blind that you can't even see the amount of defects impressive that a person has, you are so blind that all defects you see as something that can be improved or you fall in love with them. If someone told you that that person was worthless, you would immediately go on the defensive trying to counteract everything by saying things that make the person feel valuable. When an object is very precious to you, you take care of it, you protect it, you give it more meaning.

I remember once with my grandmother that we began to draw, she began to draw a hen, a tree, a chick and then she gave each drawing a name, for me it was a very special moment, it is one of the most beautiful memories I have with my grandmother. She, although she was not a great draftsman, made some very beautiful drawings, for me they were special, when we finished I saved the drawings, she always used to write the date and the dedication, it was very special to be honest. I remember that some time passed and when my grandmother was gone, she used to look at the sheet with the drawings to remember it, that sheet she kept very well, she took great care of it and she used to put it in a place where it was rare for it to be lost or damaged. It is likely that if the drawings were seen by some person, it would have no value, since they were drawings without any meaning: a hen, a tree and a chick, it is so much that if a person saw the drawings they would think that the person is learning to draw, or if someone found the sheet in the street, they would pass by, or maybe they would take it and throw it away (I am not discrediting my grandmother's drawings obviously, but in reality it is very likely that that would happen if I lost the sheet) People would do that because it has no value for them, nor a meaning, but for me it has a lot of value because my grandmother did it, and it has a great meaning because we made the drawings in a very funny moment, I would pay a lot of money for that sheet if I know get lost, because it is important to me.

That value that I give to the drawing is the same value that someone gives himself when he has a high self-esteem. When someone has high self-esteem, it is a person who values himself, as he knows that he exists, he gives the applause that he has to give, he is someone who when people try to sink him does not need to prove anything, he knows what he is worth and therefore withdraws of those people. It is curious to hear that many people when they are insulted or discredited try to equal themselves by thinking that they have high self-esteem, this is a deception, what really happens is that since what others said about you hurts you, you put yourself at the same height, height that there is not of course, you have to lower yourself to equalize, causing you to lose your horizon level, when you equalize now with the person reacting to what he has said you are showing that what he said hurts so much that you have to react, this makes conclude that your self-esteem is so low that anyone destabilizes you, so you go on the defensive.

Imagine that I was born in such a country "X" and a lot of people arrive and tell me that I am not from that country "X" that I am from another, a certain "Y". If I defend my position, what happens is that what they said deep down I believe it, it is true and that is why it destabilizes me, so my reaction is: -I defend it-. If mothers were worth what they said, why do I have to defend him? —Aaahh I'm from another country, that's fine — nothing happens. The mind can be very deceptive if you do not know yourself, making you believe that you are defending a position without knowing that you are sinking in mud.

So in order to focus on self-esteem, builds, feeds every day, is formed, as we have said everything is: PROCESS. We will see the steps to build self-esteem later. For now, let's get down to what you have to do.

When a person asks me why do you need self-esteem? I simply tell him: When you have self-esteem, everything becomes easier, being in the mountains makes you see the landscape, makes you feel great, there is nothing better in life than feeling great in front of situations, imagine feeling tiny, feeling small is be at the pantry of others, that they trample you, it is not because people are bad and want to trample you, only that when someone sees a cockroach they want to step on it, that is the same when you have low self-esteem, people can be a little heavy or mocking Tell people not to make fun of stuttering, most people laugh when someone stutters, is it that they want to make you feel bad? ---- NOOOO

--- it is simply because he does not understand stuttering, he is funny, it is something that he does not usually live, that is why people laugh or turn their eyes to not see you, what you think from then on is Your problem, with high self-esteem that slips you because you know your worth, because that mockery is a blowjob for you, you are so big that you would waste your time seeing the cockroach that speaks to you in front of you.

You have to feel like you're in the clouds, eagles are animals that I love because they always fly high up, when the storm hits the other birds hide to take refuge, but the eagle draws strength and flies higher finding winds that favor it. The code of the eagle is: -live high-fly high and die high-you will never see an eagle walking around. The same as a person with high self-esteem, you will never see him discredit himself or say: -How sorry for me that I have a stutter-. Look, if you have to look at the whole little world, do it, I don't care, what matters is that you build yourself, if someone tells you that you are very egocentric, it is still around, it is better to feel like a lion than an ant.

Life is to look giant, look at everyone like ants if you have to, I don't give a damn if you behave then as egocentric, but YOU WILL HAVE TO DO EVERYTHING TO ACQUIRE A SELF-ESTEEM FROM THE CLOUDS. You are a lion in the jungle, lions are not compared to anyone, you will never see a lion measuring himself against an ant, he does not need that, he knows he is a lion, the other companions, life is yours, you are what matters most. You live this life, others will always be mere traveling companions, no one buries with anyone, my friend, because you will lower your self-esteem with me if I will not be willing to bury myself with you on the day of your death. You do not have to give value to anyone, you can give it and that's fine, we are human beings who value things or people, but never give the other more value than you, when you give value you give it away, the power you give is the one you should give yourself first.

When someone has power he infects others, he does not need to give it, it is something that comes naturally. When you have a high self-esteem you will have so much that it will be seen through your veins, you will walk differently, your posture will change, your language will be transformed, you will speak confidently with your words, you will feel firm, abundant, you will be the TOP of the ideal man in anything. The world constantly needs people with that high self-esteem, most people have a low self-esteem and that is a great advantage for you, because the world loves confident and self-confident people. You will hear things like: "Companies hire people who know, people fall in love with others because of their personality, people love to be with others because of their way of being" (all those are blowjobs, you know) companies, people, Raimundo and Everyone deep down what they want is to surround themselves with people with high self-esteem, people want to be inspired, touched, changed, transformed, you will never see insecure or fearful people behind other people with insecurities or fears, that is ridiculous, a The blind never leads the blind (that's silly) they want someone to see the way, the same is with people.

Imagine how rich it would be when people follow you, when everyone sees a high confidence in you that they want to imitate you, that they talk about you, that they say that person speaks security, that person knows what they want, that they tell you up front: -I know that you will do it because you denote so much confidence in you that I can believe that you will do whatever it takes to get there-. Imagine that people smell your courage, they will want to be like magnets with you, they will want to suffocate you from what you have, but deep down only you will know that you have built yourself, that it has been the whole mental process that has taken you to that level.

Remember that seeing at height is always the best !! I have had low self-esteem and high self-esteem and I would choose all my life to have my self-esteem through the roof without hesitation, because when I have a high self-esteem I can make people follow me in quantity, I can help others, make books, conferences, coaching, videos, leadership, travel the world inspiring people, I can do all that and it feels great when you make others watch In the height. You never want to be down, it is more difficult to climb, why do you think that when people get lost in a desert they look for a mountain to climb? Because from there you can see the way forward, they can also see you there to rescue you, because from there you clarify the panorama. The same is with stuttering when you climb the mountain you clarify the process of overcoming, you know where to go, but if you have a trampled self-esteem, how can you see the road if you are buried there?

The Approval of Others

We come to the hottest topic !! Yes! Yes! Yes! I deeply believe that if you have this very clear concept uffffffff, you are going to make a painting of the world! I do not know why it happens that when people overcome this of the approval of others, the stuttering process is a piece of cake (LITERAL) see that is the first literal I do in CAPITAL LETTER, I really know how important this is. What's more, I could say that if you want the rest you can do it over low heat, but you have to have this injected into the jugular vein, not being more, let's get into the matter.

"The approval of others" mmmmm see I do not know where to start, does the phrase say it alone, right? Is there something that has knocked down more dreams, lives, ideals, loves ... than this concept ...? This phrase is like a virus that when it hits you it ends, you feel that you are living normal but deep down you are fried.

If you saw that most people have this virus, seriously when it hits you it is very difficult to release it, it is like gum that chases you. Like everything we have seen, first, to know if you have this problem since this could be considered a big problem, you will have to analyze yourself deeply, ask yourself what happens in your daily life, when I talk to someone I get nervous? When we are in a family reunion I feel uncomfortable? Do I constantly tend to put the other person above me? Do I feel discomfort when they ask me? In an exhibition to the public do I get nervous? If I see someone important who speaks to me, do I get paralyzed? When I expose myself to many people, I feel super uncomfortable? Am I afraid to speak? Do I live thinking about the opinion of others? Do I constantly look at events in my life with people's eyes as if I were them to see how I was? Or if I stutter a lot? Or what idea did they take from me? Do I always want to look good to others? Is the opinion of others important to me? I don't care about the opinion of others, just that I don't like to make a fool of myself? .....etc etc....

97

If your answer to any of the previous questions is yes, it does not matter if it is only in one, let me tell you my dear friend that you have the virus, I am sorry. The good thing is that you have it and you have noticed, the bad thing is that it is still there and you have to remove that cavity once and for all.

I will tell you how bad you will go in this life if you continue to depend on the opinions of others. When you go to make your dreams come true, you will not do it because you will think that people will laugh if you fail, before you start something your loved ones will come to tell you, do you really want to do it? And you as a good son or nephew or whatever, you will say: -I will not do it, family, I have them on a pedestal so high that everything they say I do-. If at any time you meet a person that interests you, you will not talk to her because a thought will cross your mind that says: What will she think of me when she knows that I have a stutter? Then you will start giving yourself a thousand and one reasons not to start a conversation, and you will be so crack that you will even say: nahh he would not like it. How about that no? You will be so crack that all those thoughts you will turn them into justifications for not starting a conversation and thus not feeling guilty for not having done it because well, there are just reasons not to do it. When you are looking for a job, you won't even say the ideas you have to improve the company. Why? ... we already know ... what can your boss think of you? It's more! ... It is very likely that you will become someone else's napkin, working for others, doing things without revealing yourself, always paying attention to what any asshole tells you, going like the horses in front of you!

There are more than a thousand reasons why your life is too sad if you continue to cultivate that virus, it is that they are your dreams for the love of God, it matters more than your dreams, you will tell me: family, partner, children, of course yes, but dreams are what tie all that together, no one who has not fulfilled their dreams has their social family circle resolved, it lacks essence, you are someone else from the lot, I know these things are hard, I know, but believe me, No one will tell you like me, people will always put warm water cloths on you, or if you go to a psychologist will give you hot water so that you can go through things without pain, but nooo, in this life you have to be REALISTIC and reality is that everything they have told you about looking good in front of people is an absurd lie.

Since we were little they have taught us to behave as others say, to always look good, to be that wonderful boy, how many times do we not hear that at school that says: discipline always better yeahiiii! Excelsior always more! or things from the teachers like: Don't look bad to your classmates, don't be silly up front ... etc ... or the thousand and one way they taught us to look "good" to others ... I really don't judge that society has This style is normal, we are sociable beings, that has made us evolve. ionar, peroooo... .always the but... .this has already happened, it is already an old story, that is... .we have to modernize skinny.

Today's world is: DIFFERENT. Going through life approving of others is not something really motivating ... I continue ... I tell you that I had to stop at this point to take up again with more force since I was doing some little things.

Life is yours, you are the one who has the power, in life we are born with mommy, daddy, grandmothers, uncles and a lot of people who often get in the way before helping, nothing happens, people make mistakes, the important thing is put them in their place, the ranking of this life is you, you are in the TOP-TOP TOP !! Above, from there to below, maybe you can put mmmm: YOU TOO, already when there is a tiny, tiny, tiny space ... well there if ... YOU TOO !!! Because in this life the most important thing is You !! The others are just traveling companions.

When you talk to someone you do not have to give your power to that person, they do not deserve it, people do not deserve to be giving them your power, how could you give to drink if you have not quenched your thirst? Maybe they have taught us to that we first share with others or live at the pantries of others, but that type of philosophy is very poor, it is poor in the sense that you will never really be helping anyone, the only thing you will show is fear, weakness, lack, need, When you first quench your thirst, you can already give to others because you will already have the strength to give and the desire to offer, otherwise you will show the world the need. The same thing happens when you talk to someone, if at any point in the conversation you feel that you are afraid, it bothers you, you feel bad, it makes you nervous, it hurts to stutter, deep down you are giving your approval to the other, if so You only give a pinch, a simple pinch, that you know that you are giving your approval ... you did not sell it, you gave it away.

If we put ourselves in the eyes of the other person, it is more uncomfortable when someone is afraid in a conversation, you do not know what the hell they are talking about, if you are afraid in the conversation or you value the other person there is nothing, there is a Mental struggle of your brain wanting to flee, the person in front closes in on you thinking, Why will he do that? Why does he behave like this? I want to be a little more explicit in this part.

When you are in a conversation (I speak of a conversation since it is the main way that you give power away) if you give approval to the other that you know that the other does not like that, not because he feels discomfort, I repeat ... that the other feels uncomfortable is worth a three ... but if we take it to that ... the person in front will not understand what is happening with you because that attitude of giving approval IS NOT NORMAL.

In school, as we said at the beginning, they have taught us that having Nerves is normal, I make this very clear: THAT IS NOT NORMAL. It is a blowjob invented by people which we did not eat with chips. How can it be normal for you to be nervous when talking to someone else? Maybe you say it's real, hey real if it is, that's why you feel it, but just because it's real doesn't mean it's normal, why isn't it normal? Because when you are nervous it means that you are giving approval to the other, that's why you get nervous, that's why you think that the other makes you nervous. The other or the other never makes you nervous, what makes you nervous is the IDEA that how are you in front of ANOTHER then that other depending on how you climb it (when I talk about climbing I mean that the people you know are giving them a ranking : maybe your dad makes you nervous, you put it in number 1, maybe your friend not so much, you put it in number 6, mmmm your teacher if it makes you nervous then you put it in position 2, and so on you are putting to people on a scale, obviously you do not consent, all this is something that happens without you having a clue, it happens because you sell your approval to the highest bidder ... ahiii what a shame ... give your approval to everyone ... I was wrong) Where were we going... .aaa yes... .when you get nervous you don't get nervous about the other, you get nervous because of the interpretation you have of the other.

I am talking to someone, I give him my approval (here you are already fried) we continue talking and every time I am running out of strength, obviously, for giving away my power. We talk ... we talk ... I stutter ... I stutter ... and I draw the conclusion of: -the other one makes me nervous-. First, the other does not have the power to make you feel nervous, if he does it is because you are allowing that or you get under him, although the truth is you do not put yourself under him, you put him on a pedestal (it is different) the second : what makes you nervous are the interpretations you have of that person, that person is very important, -oh my God is someone recognized- -oh is my relative- -oh is that it is a girl- -oh is that it is someone strange - -oh is that .... is that ... - ("esque" -----> typical excuse that has buried millions of dreams along with the "but" and the "why ..."
Feeling nervous is not normal, although there are situations where IF IT IS NORMAL to feel it, for example: when you declare yourself to someone you like or give the first kiss, when you are playing something important, but all that is not nerves (hahaha you fell, in truth that is not nerves)

I'll tell you something real about athletes. It is said that soccer players once when they go out on the pitch they get nervous, they are afraid, they sweat. Many players are asked why this happens and most respond that if you are not nervous before going out to play it is because you no longer like it. In sports such as soccer, the psychology of the player is handled a lot, it is said that the player is not really nervous, but that he is excited to play, he has so much intrigue about how things will be done that he enters into that emotion of power play. In these sports the nerves turn into excitement to play, it is the same emotion "nerves" but with a different approach.

What happens with stuttering is very similar, when you go up on stage two things can happen: oh that you have nerves or that you address them, not having them is weird, but having them is not normal (I know it can be weird to understand this until now but you will see it as the process progresses) when you are there in front of the public most people get nervous because we are human beings evolved as social beings and once we look at people we begin to interpret things, those things are often thoughts of: what the hell will they think of me? What do I have to say? There are many people watching me, what am I going to do? .... etc ... etc ... etc ... at that moment the thoughts flutter like butterflies making you feel nervous and generating reactions such as spasms, you stay quiet, you stutter more, you get lost, you talk things that they are not, you go like a flash or a thousand words per second ... etc ... etc ... the interesting thing at this point is to realize that the nerves are stupid ... but if you can't control them then try to focus them as passion or excitement from public speaking.

The best coaches or people who speak in public I include myself, what we usually do is focus our nerves ---> towards motivation and enjoy how great it is to speak for the public, being very clear that: "what others think it's worth three hectares of shit "---------------> tattoo this very well

Once I remember that a great coach was asked if it was the same to speak in front of 10 people than to speak in front of a million people, he answered in a very curious way: You know, that question is asked a lot and what I am going to do. Saying may not seem like it, but it is true, it is completely the same to speak to 10 people than to a million. The journalist who asked him was very doubtful and added: why do you say that if a million are many eyes looking at you? The coach replied: for that same reason is that you have not given a lecture to a million people (audience laughter) most people focus on what others may think, but I always focus on what I can give to the rest, for that reason 10 people is irrelevant to me than a million.

What the coach said above is true, it does not matter completely, the only difference is in what you can think of the context. When there are 10 people you can say to yourself: well there are only 10 people, but when there are a million you could say to yourself: oh my God there are 1 MILLION !! It does not matter exactly the same when your mind is well grounded, the others, whether en masse or group, it does not matter, it will always be the same result because the only thing that can change that is in your mind.

This concept is not to talk about how to speak in public, it is about stuttering, but we know that stuttering has a lot of fabric in this space of public speaking because it touches the fibers of others.

The conclusion that we could draw and that I would like you to get out of your head is that nobody makes you nervous, you get nervous when you talk to x or y person. Nobody takes away your power, you give it power by giving it away. No one is more important than you ... you put them on a pedestal. You do not stutter when you are with another in front, your interpretations of thinking that there is another make you stutter with that person.

If I am honest with you as I have always been in this book, it is that most stuttering is social, seriously, indeed, it is sad to say it really, one would like it to be something else, some therapy, hypnosis, "method", recipe , something that is out there very deep, but there is not ... have you asked yourself why is there not? Well, for the simple reason that it doesn't exist. If you really take the issue of the approval of others very seriously, I think that from now on you will be a machine, you will break every friend, you will be incredible, what's more, I don't even tell you how far you could go.

I like to tell people that to remove the approval of others you first need to get a tattoo on your head: I DON'T GIVE A FUCK WHAT PEOPLE THINK ABOUT ME. This is one of the things that we will go into more later.
thoroughly but now I would like us to make it clear. It might sound vulgar, ugly, self-centered, whatever ... I don't give a three ... do you know why? Because this life (this, this, this life) this life does not move in between, this life is not: good a little, bad a tris, or take that path and take the other at the same time, I am happy and a little sad, those things

do not happen, or you are or you are not, it is the same as I say: I do not care a three what you think of me, but what I do assure you is that if you take this seriously you will thank me a lot because it is the only way out.

In short: that you give a shit, a reverend shit what others think of you, that you give a shit, if someone were to comment on you, someone thinks about you, someone looks at you, someone laughs at you, Well, you spend it with toilet paper (LITERAL) (LITERAL) (LITERAL) you take the toilet paper and start to write down all the people who give them approval and you pass it there and throw it away as it should be.

It is the only way out of the doors of Overcoming, when you stop caring what others think of you is when you start to really live life.

It was thought that most people left this life without regret, although it was found that people actually left with many regrets, especially one very in contract.

Long time working Australian nurse Bronnie Ware, a terminally ill intensive care nurse, mentioned in her famous book "Honest and Frank Confessions of People on Their Death Beds" the main regret of most terminally ill people.

"The main regret of many people is: " 'I wish I had the courage to do what I really wanted to do and not what others expected me to do,'" she added in her famous book.

It is sad to think that this is the typical phrase that people say before they die, but it is not strange to think that it is not this, for the reason that most people suffer from the virus of the approval of others. I have had the opportunity to work on the stuttering process with older people and it is a privilege to hear when they say: I started living at 60 years old, I started to be happy at 45 years old, I knew what I was 73 years old. it was freedom.

Because deep down when you put the opinion of others aside and give yourself power, you really start to be happy. It is not only that this virus destroys your self-esteem, it really destroys all your dreams, be-cause when you want to do something then you will not do it, why? By-the-probation-of-others.

Later we will focus on the steps to leave the approval of others, for now it is "HHobligatory" with double "HH" that you understand the impor-tance of being worth the opinion of others, hey why are you going to approve the others If they do not live life for you, understand that, what do you gain by giving the other a power that is yours, it was born from you, the beings that have really left would be very sad if you every time you go out there you give away your power by giving the another approv-al, the other does not deserve that, that is yours, and it is too valuable to give it, I will leave you a great reflection that I love:

"If you are not willing to bury yourself with me on the day of my death, you have no reason to think about me"

People are not going to bury themselves with you, they don't have to, hey, it's your life, you're the asshole who gives approval, not them, so don't feel angry when giving approval. When you talk to someone and you stutter and think that it is because of the other, do not be angry with him, be angry with yourself for having validated the other without deserving it.

The following could be called as the sermon of freedom, I would like that once you read it from time to time (every p. Day, hopefully every p. Day you read that sermon)

Freedom Sermon:

"I am a Being that does not give a damn about the approval of others, I look in front, to the sides, at me in front of the mirror, then I look at everyone and tell them: what you think of me I don't give a shit, three hectares of shit and shit what you think of me. I am a being that when conversing with other people I don't care what they are thinking, what they say, what they whisper, I only care what I say, because I understand that I love myself and I am the owner of my life, like The owner of my life, I send to hell whoever I like.

I am a being that when I express myself in public I express myself in the best way since I do not care about three peppers what others are seeing, thinking or hearing from me. I do it because I have a great time that I am the center of attention, that people talk about me ha-ha-ha I laugh because I know that I am a wonderful being, and if they talk about me let them talk, because the day they don't talk I will wonder why the hell are they not talking? I know it's free publicity when people talk about me.

I am a being that in the first position I am, of second and or, from third to me, from there to the bottom, well me too, the others are unfortunately not in this row, they are ... no idea ... I am a being that the truth is that I don't give a fucking shit what people think of me, I have that tattooed on my skin. "

This type of mentality is the mentality that successful people have, great people, do you think they are thinking about the opinion of others? Nooo, obviously noo, that is too small, that is depressing, what a weariness of intelligence in something as silly as: having as I think for others to approve of me. It's too much of a waste for successful people, what's more, these types of people live their ordinary lives by getting people to talk about them.

There is a very particular case that happened once with the soccer player named Neymar, this player usually had a time where people made fun of him for the way he was thrown in each game, for some he was a clown, for others ridiculed soccer, and others he was a magician. Unfortunately, there was a time when this player was highly criticized by the media, the press and people were angry when he played, but what was most striking was that this player had become the most searched player on the internet, the most awarded in social media and had come to the fore in the media. Although what seems most curious to me was that at the peak of being criticized this player did more things to attract attention, why? Some will think that he is a player who does not make sense ... but the players have gotten used to criticism and they know that criticism is: free publicity, that's why riding criticism is a very good trip.

The same thing happens with stuttering, I used to be angry that they talked about stuttering, or that they made fun of stuttering, only if they commented on something about gagging, stuttering or speaking, it made me feel sorry, angry, sad. Today I join in those comments and I have a great time, I don't care because deep down I don't give a damn about the comments, so I have a good time, because I understand that I have a lot of value (self-esteem) because I love myself (acceptance) and because the truth is worth what someone thinks of stuttering or of me (zero approval of others)

I will continue talking a little more about this, you know (and maybe the importance of this topic) I will touch on the subject of how it is to treat the majority of people who come to me, the truth is I like to be very honest, also sometimes rude in general , but in reality with people individually I am rather docile up to a point, I like to be demanding, what I mean with all this stuff is: -In this you cannot be weak, in what concerns the approval of others You cannot put cloths of warm water, you have to give the injection against the virus at once, in one go.

For this reason I am not very in favor of therapies, psychology, sweet things to overcome ... among others ... in this you have to be clear ... being clear gives you clarity ... continuing with what we were going, most of the people who turn to me their cases they have to do with a social aspect, I understand that stuttering is partly mental and partly physical due to the automatisms that we have created in the way we speak, but the main problem is never stuttering.

You have realized that stuttering is a mask that covers the real problem, when someone comes to me telling me that they have a stuttering problem I tell them that this cannot be possible since stuttering itself does not have the power to generate Problem, what happens is that the FORRRRM in which you look at stuttering is what causes it to generate those problems that are the approval of others… non-acceptance… low self-esteem….

Stuttering is like the earth that buries the real dead. The typical thing that a person tells me is that stuttering is the cause of everything, but it is an excuse for not seeing the approval of others. I have had many people who deny this, they deny it outright, they say that the problem really is stuttering, but it is not like that, that is not the problem, if you think that too, you are focusing things wrong, you will never be able to see what is behind it. stuttering. Just as obvious I go along with them without fighting with them, but … always "the but" … when we begin the work of approval of others curiously-curiously we realize that this is the real trigger. If you think that stuttering is your thing, how you see others that flow then you judge yourself, when you talk to others how you know you have stuttering you feel inferior, then what happens from then on is approval from others , you talk to people, family, friends and you feel uncomfortable, shy, fearful, etc …

I'll tell you what most say when it comes to me: -I find it difficult to talk to others, I feel uncomfortable- (approval) -Sometimes I speak well with my relatives but with strangers I don't- (approval of strangers) -I feel bad with my stuttering- (no Acceptance or rejection) -My friends laugh at my stuttering- (low self-esteem) -I am uncomfortable stuttering in front of the other- (low self-esteem + approval) -My parents were to blame for my stuttering- (approval) –I don't know what will happen to my future with stuttering- (low self-esteem) -I always think about my stuttering- (zero acceptance) -I just want to be normal- (zero acceptance) -I get very frustrated as others speak well- (zero self-esteem) -I am sorry to talk to others- (approval) - I stutter a lot when I talk to my grandfather- (approval) -I don't stutter so much when I talk to my friends- (approval anyway, when you have zero approval you stop Ranking Remember that ranking is positioning people depending on the approval you give them)

If you have any of these "problems" "doubts" "intrigues" "questions" you already know you have, needless to say. If you take a good look at everything that surrounds stuttering, it is around these three aspects: approval, acceptance, self-esteem. I find it very funny how many people in the world of stuttering: the wise men, or the "experts" talk about stuttering as if it were a panacea, something hidden there in the darkness that is difficult to decipher, which encompasses the concept, the meta-phor like the synapse, things, nonsense bullshit to give more beauty to the concept: "stuttering." But that you and I know that that little-little stuttering, is more the sweet, the position as the ranking that has been given for years since in truth it has neither ranking nor value, it is simply a mask hiding the true essence , an essence that they teach us badly since childhood.

Imagine a small child being taught with this type of reality, it is not phi- losophy of life, fuck it (I'm sorry, but more than one has told me that blowjob) this is being REALISTIC, if you think it is philosophy tell me where is the philosophical Here, where is what is not real, show me on a well-founded basis that what I have said is not true. What I say is logical, it is scientific, it is rational and it is realistic. Now imagine again a child who is taught that what others think has to matter to him five, his self-esteem has to be in the clouds and he has to completely accept, love, respect and feel proud for who he is. Do you think that a child with that ability would have time to wonder, am I really worth it? —Nooo ---. We ask ourselves that, we were taught differently, well, I no longer ask myself those questions, it is ridiculous, a while ago I gave myself the injection against that virus, it is your turn, you have to be your own teacher, your guide, your Zensei. Neither is it to see society as bad or the educational system, but you realize that some things take a looooooooo ooooooooooooooooooooooooooooooo way to improve them or it doesn't suit them. Do you think it is normal for a child to be nervous about ex- posing his classmates? Does a child with stuttering hide, feel bad, hold back, walk away? –Nooooo- that's very sad, it's to turn the school upside down, how is that possible !! to turn the parents upside down as well or the people who are teaching them that ... You have to reconsider, realize that you are focusing badly and begin to eat some principles that will serve the child for life.

I love the maxim that says: Principles are principles and will always remain principles. These tips that I give you will always remain valid, years may pass and they will always be there, we may now have technology, the digital world, the wow-wow-wow of the media, it will be the same in the digital age, now people have afraid to comment, give an opinion, congratulate, write a point of view about something, why? For that very reason…. "Others" & "low self-esteem" & "zero acceptance"

Reflect on it ... you will see that almost the greatest problem in life lies in these three pillars, Buddha already said that happiness comes from detaching yourself and when you detach yourself from the approval you have of others and when you detach yourself from an image that you think that It is the ideal and not the one you have now and when you detach yourself from a low self-esteem because having low self-esteem is not of human beings, that will make you very happy, eternally happy.

The Language

The language, although it does not fall within the main aspects that make up the Overcoming, plays an important role in promoting the overcoming in scale or what we had previously called exponential growth. The process of overcoming it could be said that it is as if you overthrow your opponent in boxing, he does not fall because of the blow you give him, it can happen, although most boxers are knocked out by the amount of blows they received from their opponent. When the ants defend their territory from invading insects or an animal, what they do is hang onto the insect and start to sting in many places, some of these bite on the head, legs, abdomen, and so on ... until in the end the invading insect falls due to the amount of bites it has.

The same happens with stuttering, the more fields you tackle in overcoming the faster, simpler and easier you can get out of all those false beliefs. I know how to make ants, try to sting various points keeping in mind the points that you must sting the most, then you will see little by little how the opponent becomes weaker, which in this case would be your old paradigms.

Returning to language, we are going to focus on two types of language, which are the body and the spoken. In this first topic we will focus on body language. There are many people (as nothing strange) (when I say few people it will be very strange) who go through life as if they were carrying bundles of cement or sacks, I think that we have all had to carry bundles on the back or on the man and we know that When we are walking with these bundles our posture is crouched, tired and we just want to get there and rest from what we are carrying. Well, likewise, there are people who go through life as if they carried double their weight, this what it does is denote fatigue, heaviness, weakness, hurt, a series of things that someone could refute: -but I do not feel that way, It is my position. Let's stop pulling and be serious, that way of communicating with others with your body is the same as your mind is believing.

When we go through life taking out a suitcase (suitcase means with a curved back) or we go through life with our head bowed, we are telling the world that it can pass us by, that we are easy prey, that life weighs so much on us that we walk that way. Look, you can have a back, neck or head problem and you could understand why you walk like this, but if you don't have any of that it doesn't give you any right to go through life that way, because when we go like this We have lost our courage, maybe you do not think you are worth little if you walk like this or go through life with that posture, but people will not give you confidence and your mind will begin to believe that this life weighs a lot.

I really like to give the example of footballers because soccer is a sport of many emotions for both the footballers and the fans who watch it, and to a large extent winning a game is not only measured by skill but by attitude. When a player enters with desire, dog, strength, courage, it is very likely that he will make a very good football game, but if he enters with his head down, arms dropped, neck curved, back curved, it is because he has lost the will to play . If you take a good look at footballers like Cristiano Ronaldo or Leonel Messi they always have a firm stance, because they know what they are worth, they know what they are, they know what they represent, they always have their gaze higher than the horizon line, only when they are losing or they have played badly, they lower their heads, which should not be done either, you should always try to keep your forehead high, your head firm, your arms firm, your back straight and show a sexy, confident posture and want to take over the world .

It is said that the most important thing about a person in the first contact with another is an interview, work, love, is: "PRESENCE": this that is not so valuable, nor is it commonly mentioned is what makes a person closes a millionaire business to another who fails in it, this so simple is what makes someone able to conquer the woman or man of their dreams and the other person cannot. That so simple is what makes people want to surround themselves with you, to look for you, to want to be with you, this simple word like "PRESENCE" collects everything that has to do with being someone who is confident, with self-esteem, of character, firm , trustworthy, everything ... this is the result of having everything focused: a PERFECT presence.

It is also said that confident people are generally those who have a look higher than the front gaze, make a trial of looking straight ahead, now tilt your head up a bit, that's how confident people look, for What you should maintain that position, I know that at first everything costs, obviously, everything is a process, obviously, but in the end your mind will believe that story, remember that after all life is the story you tell yourself.

Once I heard how a coach spoke about something particular and it was that he used to come to class at the university and see boys as they point to the people who passed by, usually they were male boys who gave scores to women. When a pretty girl passed her they said to each other: -mmmm I give that one a 5- the other said: -nooo what's up, I give that one a 2- ... and they continued like this with all the girls who passed by. The coach commented that all of us could really go down the street with a score: you are a 5 or 7, that person who goes around fallen, with his shoulders down is a 3, that person who goes with his head up, head signature, upright back that denotes security is a 10, and so we could score each person who passes by us.

It strikes me that we go through life with a score either bad, good or excellent, and that score is what people see, that we transmit to others, it is not just a question of posture, that is ridiculous, it is something you give to others is how you show yourself, what you want to communicate to the other. We all know ... you know that deep down we want to convey security, some asshole could tell you no, that he is not interested in any of that, but here you and I know that it is. This is like when we were in school and the one who went the worst at school said that he felt good, when in reality nobody wants to be the last, everyone wants to be at the top or in the middle or perhaps at the bottom but never the last, deep inside of us we want to look good, it is not to look good to others, it is something more personal, it says when we are at the end it says a lot about us, when we have those positions ourselves with ourselves we also point out, of course we do not see it but people have an idea of themselves, it can be good, average or bad, that depends largely on the self-esteem you have. What is very curious very curious is that people without high self-esteem go through life with an absolute presence! That when you see them you say WOW what security.

In general, try to maintain a firm posture, that will give you confidence. In the evolution of the human being from -homo erectus to homo sapiens- we see a very large difference in posture, the human being already stands firm, stands on his two feet, I understand that we come from animals but we have become a kind of a unique value (this here is really very subjective, what I try to focus on is the posture) Also keep your shoulders firm, not so high but natural, that they flow, but that they are not sagged as if life No matter what a three, keep your head up granting greatness, confidence, looking higher than the horizon in search of dreams, to win, to eat the world, to surpass yourself, the look higher denotes a great self-esteem, then walk with a firm step, There are people who walk as if they were blown away by the wind or others as from one side to the other, some with a tired walk, others soft as if they were floating, there are so many ways of walking that they do not give you anything, the best way to walk is safety, take firm steps (not so that you walk like the military or hitting the floor... .you understand me right?... well...)

There are many other aspects such as the look, the smile, the hands when you talk. Many ask me how the posture of the hands should be when speaking and the truth is that this is very relative, do not believe people when they tell you that moving your hands are symptoms of being nervous or shy, Or that moving a lot when you expose is fear, things like that ... the truth is that everyone takes their own postures in the hands or movements, what is true from my experience is that moving the hands makes it easier to get more emotions, for me it is more easy to make myself understood with my hands, of course I don't think it is easier to make myself understood, I like it and I find it interesting, that's why I do it, then it makes it easy for me to explain myself with the movements of my hands. There are many famous people, successful people, entrepreneurs who communicate a lot with their hands, it is something natural. What I think is that the best way to communicate is by taking advantage of the greatest possible tools and your hands is something very cool to take advantage of.

Now in terms of the look, the gestures or gesticulations as it is commonly called should be focused on transmitting security, on giving confidence, if you are going to smile: --- smile big ---- that your brain understands that you are smiling, There is a scientific fact that I read once that said that when we smile even though we don't want to, the brain thinks you are happy. After this I thought: -clearly everything in life is about fooling the brain-. If your mind thinks that you are unhappy, it begins to trick it into believing that you are happy and so your brain will eat that story. That is why you will hear me a lot say that the story you tell yourself is the one that has the greatest weight in the end, if you have a story that is sad, it does not benefit you, you tell it and you get frustrated, try to change that story, add interesting parts to it, focus on the most valuable thing in the story, what makes you build, change the story to a story that you are proud to tell it as if it were a Hollywood movie where the story ends with the best happy endings, fool your brain, the things we are seeing from language, from words, from the mind, all of this is fooling your mind, change those old obsolete things that do not work and give it an injection of what Again, it's what will get you far.

It is also common for people to tell me that they cannot keep their eyes on people, if you have read the above in detail you will know that this excuse is one of the three main problems, I would categorize it as "approval of others + self-esteem" in These two may be, if someone does not keep their gaze avoiding it, they are simply giving approval to the other, it may be clear that ... there are certain people who do not look at the eyes, it is normal, they do not look because they do not want to, or they look for a while (although do not look at any moment of the conversation if it is very strange) that transmits a lot of insecurity, and it does not matter if it is transmitted or not, remember that this is not about focusing on others, the important thing is how you feel, I understand that this stage I speak a lot about language about transmitting to others, but really deep down what you are is what you transmit. A passage from the bible said: -do not be like the Pharisees who have an impure heart and do good works, first clean the cup inside so that it shines on the outside-. That's true, you know, what you are inside shines on the outside, because maintaining a facade of what you are not does not last long, people will know later the colors you paint.

So keeping a glance is synonymous with security? mmmm it is relative but it is better to keep it, why? ... who the heck are you talking to then ... one as a listener would like to be looked at one in the eyes, also when one is speaking he would like to be seen in the eyes too, is How to pay attention, in any case you will know that, you are the one who knows why the hell you do not look into the eyes, but I tell you that there is nothing like looking into the eyes, after all, the eyes are the door of the soul , It sounds philosophical but seeing a person in the eye and talking to him has to be something that you see beautiful, safe people speak directly to you, look you in the eye, I don't know if you have heard someone say to you: -look me in the eye- -look at me when I talk to you- that person doesn't do it because you want you to look at him, he says it because he wants to be honest, because he wants to tell you things directly, so think about all those things.

Once I was in the gym, the truth is I did not know much about the GYM, I started cycling or what is known as elliptical, then some tread-mill, basic exercises, things like that. There was a coach who was there who decided to train me, I saw how the people in the gym made a lot of effort in the weights, running on the elliptical, I saw how most of the people showed that strength in their faces, in the demand and I it seemed something very particular. When I trained with him we started doing simple exercises, something that I will always remember was when he said to me: -Do you see all those people who exercise? - I said: -Yes of course, you can see the desire-. He told me: -it's not desire, it's effort, but effort is not synonymous with work, when you do the exercises try to make them "SEXY", make them look "SEXY" because that way you will see how you enjoy it more-. When he told me this I understood ev-erything, in life you have to try to make everything look sexy (hahahaha it sounds funny but if you saw how real it is) when I started doing the exercises I tried to make them look sexy, that I see myself sexy, the way I took the weights, raised them, of doing the treadmill that saw me as a Hollywood actor, and the truth was I enjoyed it so much, I felt how people looked at me and said: -what an interesting boy- others said: - he does the exercises very well - but actually it was a thought that made everything around me great. When I saw how my coach did the exercises, heck !! He was a guy who enjoyed exercising like never before, but the most fascinating thing was that he did very sexy exercises (I say it with all due respect of course) he drew people's attention, obviously someone could say that he was a coach but no, his mentality was different Unlike the majority who made faces of pain, grotesque gestures, screams, the guy did it "sexy" he had the mentality that when he did the exercises he would do them well, that if someone looked at him he would say: -Wow, you notice how he exercises, he likes to exercise.

This story comes to mind when I talk about body language, when you start to take care of your body language think: "how do I look sexy?" If you are not capable, I recommend that you see the actors, they know in very well handle this concept. You have seen when women go out on the catwalk: they know that they are beautiful and they know that they have to walk with style, the same when men in the movies walk with a firm step, their gaze is serene, you can tell, you hear people who say: I would like to be like that actor or like this other and so, more than his beauty is the style, it is knowing how to be SEXY.

I know the topic above is something that some might say is out of context but nooo, do you know why? because most of the people who come to me are typical people who hide, they are afraid, they walk with their heads down, they look at the ground, they think they are horrible, they think they are the worst thing, low self-esteem, they have bored facial expressions, their face denotes tiredness, all those things, all for the simple reason that they haven't realized that their body language is a reflection of who they are on the inside.

At first I understand that it will cost you a bit… ..hey I understand… because it is as if it were not you… as if you were doing another role… I understand it… .but in this life we are always playing a role, really the authenticity It is something that goes inside, you do not speak the same with your partner as with your grandmother, or you behave the same, to each person you are a little different, we are many roles at all times, nothing happens, now if you want to be the same role Nothing always happens man, nothing happens, the only problem here is not realizing how you are to be able to change, that is sad, because if you can change and you don't do it for a reason, let me tell you that reason why not You do it is what everyone wakes up to when they come to me, because for each thing there is: --------- an excuseaaa !!! Exactly !!! BINGO-BINGO-BINGO !! AN EXCUSE!!

So do not worry if it is not you, or you make a character, then we will see this in depth, the important thing is to trick your brain. Always remember this statement, I leave you with this great bold reflection for you to tattoo on your skin:

"The water does not pierce the rock for its hardness but for its constancy"

Steps to Acceptance - Self Esteem - Zero Approval

It is necessary to understand (reviewing a little what has been seen previously) that thoughts, emotions and words are created with habits, remember the maxim that says:

Cultivate a thought and you will cultivate an action, cultivate an action and you will cultivate a habit, cultivate a habit and you will cultivate a lifestyle.

This section was going to be fully developed, but thinking about it I left it at the end to close with a flourish everything that is Overcoming + Correction since as I told you at the beginning it is something that goes hand in hand, Obviously Overcoming is everything , but correction is something that will empower you.

We know that the change of improvement occurs when you handle these three aspects to perfection plus a fourth that would be the language of both words and body language. First we will see what the correction is and then do the steps together, remember that at the beginning I had also told you that the actions are what materialize, well, the steps have to do with actions, reflections, imitations, things for your Mind change to the new you, in the end all this is for you to get the new YOU, which will be the best version you have ever met on the face of the earth.

There is a very interesting concept about Egyptian scarabs: The Egyptians worshiped or had the scarab as a reference, why the scarab? Some might say that it is a harmless insect, even clumsy, with nothing to do, but the beetle for the Egyptians meant the constant change in life, everything in nature is changing, life, death, night, morning, Back then the Egyptians gratified what happened in nature, they did not oppose it as is often done now with death or natural things.

The beetle is an insect that buries itself in the sand at night and comes out at dawn with the first rays of the sun, so the beetle represented that constant change that is good for nature, that "rebirth" that makes things reborn everything time. This concept is important because change is natural, it is good, you have to receive it with open arms to do wonderful things with life.

There is a mythological animal that always caught my attention, surely you have heard him speak and it is the phoenix, this is a kind of mythological god bird that lives a long life, but before dying it makes a show of flames remaining in the ashes of the which are reborn, the most interesting thing is that the phoenix is not the same again, it is different from the previous one. Legend has it that the phoenix is reborn from time to time from the ashes or bones of its predecessor. This mythological narrative has a lot to do with our life, when people change they really do not become the same again, life is constant change, it is equal to the similarity that towards the great philosopher Heraclitus: No one bathes twice in the same river, Although "apparently" the river is the same, its elements, its course, the water that runs through it have changed.

If I saw a photo of me as a child or from several years ago before I had overcome stuttering, that is not me, that is not really me, that was someone else, I am different, there I would think very differently, if I were to speak back in the past with that person it would definitely not be me, I would think so differently, the body would be so different. I understand

119

the concept of "Youth" or that there I was "so many years" or that this is me in my past, but if you start to be realistic, -that's not me-, that child in that photo has such a mentality different that now it's not me. Nor do I say it in a term of rejection, some years ago, although I had another way of thinking, I do not reject that now because I have another way of thinking, nor when I say that it is not me, I say it for other reasons, actually as we said At the beginning we all change, nature is changing, that's why that child that you were before or a year ago was not you, if you brought that person that you were a few years ago, he would think differently, he would do things differently, he would make different decisions, you would really be another. So what I want to tell you is that we have the ability to change and don't believe the idea that you are playing another role, every day in each situation we put on different masks.

Later we will see very in depth the steps that would be the actions to be carried out in Overcoming and correcting stuttering.

Stuttering Correction

When we talk about stuttering correction we have to remember what we talked about above; Did I tell you that the overcoming is 80% and the correction is 20%? also that there is no person that I (I repeat) that I know who has not gone through improvement first.

All people who CORRECT their stuttering go through overcoming. But ... always "the but" ... does not mean that the correction is worth mothers ... that ... you heard ... that it is worth mothers ... not at all. Correction of stuttering is as important as improvement, but what I recommend is to do everything at the same time. When we talk about the exercises, which is practically one with many ramifications, the ideal is to do everything together, not one little thing first, then the other, then the other, noooo ... that's stupid.

Pretend as if you were a player of some sport. Do you think they train a certain part of the body? –NOOO- They train various parts of the body, warm up, then exercise in different parts, do exercises to exercise certain muscles, they do everything in the same day and they repeat it every day constantly. The best athletes, even if they have a highly developed talent, have their other characteristics very well perfected, otherwise they would only be good with something special. Let's take the example of Messi, we know that this player is a great dribbler (who can take several players with the ball) this I think is his maximum ability, but his other abilities such as having a good reading of the terrain, hitting the ball, passing, etc ... etc ... they are excellent. If he were not like that, he would be a guy who reggazes and that's it, but all those other qualities do not exist because, it is because he "he" has trained them.

Likewise, how we will do all the actions of the hand, all in one, complete package, tick-tack - tick tack –tick-tack. You have to be a machine at this.

Now siiiiiiiii --THE STUTTLE CORRECTION--. When we are little one of the things they teach us is to speak, but have you ever wondered how they teach us to speak? The way in which they teach us to speak is by pronouncing simple words such as: ma-ma or pa-pa, hence the child begins to unify the letters into words, so the first thing we learn is to say sounds, when we are surprised by something we say : oh-oh-oh ... or when the child calls his mother: ma-mmmmm-ma-mmmm after this the child composes his sounds into words: pa-pa ... ho-la ... and with this union of words the child is composing short sentences without adding connecting words or other more complex ones.

We must understand that our learning goes from sounds through letters and joining words ending with sentences. That's the whole stage of learning, something really basic. It must also be said that the child usually learns by example in a simpler way, when we look at a baby, his parents are constantly telling him to say the word mommy or daddy ... the child doesn't really think to say Those things, parents believe that if and that is where they begin to say things like that their son is intelligent or certain blowjobs, but in reality what the baby does is repeat, a child learns by example, remember this well (a child learns with the EXAMPLE) then the child acts like a mirror, I don't know if you have played hide and seek with the child, he adopts that same position, and that is something more of evolution, we human beings cannot forget that we are social beings With mirror features, what others do you are likely to do to feel part of the herd. Obvious today things have changed but those mirror neurons (like the actions of others) are there imitating the behaviors of the people around us.

There are many who ask me if a boy is born with stuttering parents, will he stutter? That really has two answers, although in the first place the boy is not born with a stutter, nobody is born with a stutter that I know from my own experience and that of many stutterers that I have known, none are born being a stutterer, that is my position, I also respect Those who think so, although I respect that position that I duuuuudoo looooong, secondly, if you are not born a stutterer you "are" a stutterer.

Looking at the question from my experience, you can be a stutterer and not be, when a child is born with stuttering parents they will teach him to speak, practically the first words or the first communication contact of the child are his parents, it is very likely that the child start to stutter because as we said before the boy does everything his parents do, therefore as his parents speak the child will take that way of speaking, that the truth if we are honest stuttering is simply a strange way of speaking so to speak (I say this to simplify the whole stuttering thing that in the end is a way of talking that we create point) or ede that the child does not take that way of speaking and takes the way of speaking of his classmates, teachers or people around him.

You have to understand that the child is a reflection of what his parents are, if he sees that his parents stutter, he will begin to create automatisms and he will think that this is the way to speak. Also if you put yourself in the place of the father when he talks to him or communicates to him, he will say it by stuttering, the child will see how his father speaks to him and will take that idea. Peroooo this may not happen as it has also been in many cases that children do not adopt stuttering, because they begin to speak without creating those repetitions or automatisms that we have talked about, then they speak often, also the context that we already said as people external to their parents can influence.

It's funny because many people, friends of mine, told me that when they had a stuttering friend, the words would start to stick to him, it was something very funny since it had never happened to them, they told me that they also got tongue-tied. Imagine if you "spoke fluently" and all people were stutterers, it is obvious, logical, rational, scientific, whatever ... the words are going to start to stick to you ... and it is scientific that you end up speaking in the same way, they say and this is true that you are the sum of the 5 people around you.

Understanding a little how a child's learning is, you have to know that when the child begins to say the first words or form sentences, then he is taught to vocalize, because his sounds of both letters such as r, s , the m, they sound strange, then the modulation of the words begins to be perfected.

For example, in my case I used to say the letter "R" as an "L" it is very easy to get entangled with these words and to this day we see how many instead of saying words that have the "R" say it as if it were a "L". One thing: this is super normal ... nothing happens ... it is not something to criticize or judge, it is simply a way of speaking, nothing more. Continuing with what we were, the child modulates the words to the point that he manages to understand what he says, not so much the accent or the way he says it but more the technicality of the word.

For example, the word: "eat" the child can begin by saying "I eat it" and the adult is guiding him to say: YOOO QUIE-ROO CO-MER, while he is saying this the adult is gesturing with his mouth open so that the words can be understood by the child so that the child also knows how to say it and begins to VOCALIZE (that is, to open his mouth wide by removing the sounds) the child then begins to repeat over and over and over and over again the word until he picks it up.

After the child repeats all this, he strengthens it with ... guess what? with the Readings !!! Exact with the readings. Suddenly you remember a book that they bought you as a child to learn to read, although in truth what it teaches us is to speak. There is something very curious and it is the difference that is made between reading and speaking, this seems stupid to me, I understand that reading has to do with looking at letters and talking, but when we say reading is the same as talking (you will understand this in a while) I had a certain book called "nacho lee" this book had words, some phrases and vowels, through this book I learned some things. Through constant reading, a child develops the fluency of words, the more constant he does it, the more he develops the ability to read, and so on.

I don't know if at this point you have noticed something. I'm going to make it simple and easy for you: Reading is what will make you correct stuttering (RELITERAL) Many people think of correcting stuttering with hypnosis, methods, breaths, mantras, or other ridiculous things that people make up, but the The best way to correct stuttering is with readings, and when we talk about reading I don't mean reading books:

-NOOO- that's ridiculous, I mean talking, because when we read we are talking, here at this same point you can ask yourself: But then if you tell me that, can I correct the stuttering by talking to someone else? And the answer is: -it is complex- that is, you can do it (of course, obviously) but you will not do it because there is another person in front and if you do not have the improvement well done you will not do it, although if you have the improvement and correct the stuttering by speaking It is welcome, but I, I, I repeat (I) and most of the people I know do not give to correct it from speech, that is, speaking with others (this may sound confused, but then I will explain it very well)

The difference between reading and speaking is none, you have to be clear about that, what happens is that correcting it from the readings is simpler because you manage the times, the language, you can catch the speech with your hands, when you are speaking, how on earth are you going to start creating automatisms? (Remember that automatisms are those repetitions of the new language that is going to be r creating) from the readings is that you are going to implement speech.

I repeat again because I give so much importance to the readings. I, Santiago Rave Herrera, give importance to the readings because from the readings it is that you can correct the speech since when you read (YOU SPEAK) but the most fascinating thing is that in the readings we will adopt various types of readings that you will naturally accommodate speech.

But this is not the most important thing to correct stuttering. The most important thing is to "unlearn" if exactly "unlearn" as we said up there, what we are going to do with the readings is for you to speak again. Pretend that you do not know how to speak anything, that you were born again and are as old as you are now, the most important thing is: -unlearn-, how do you unlearn? letting go of the old automatisms or paradigms of speech, I know that unlearning is complex, but it is constancy, have you ever wondered why it is easier for a child to learn? It is logical: because he does not know. When you know something and you have to change it, it takes you longer to adapt to new habits. This thing about stuttering is the same: adapting a habit of fluency that we will obtain in the readings and that will be reflected in speech.

Let us begin. It is necessary to clarify that the readings are not reading and now, it is reading intelligently, I repeat again (when I speak of reading I speak of speaking, from seeing letters: it is the same as speaking) something else to clarify and I think I should have done it at the beginning So that there are no misunderstandings is: I am not a speech therapist, I am not a speech therapist, nor am I a psychologist, but I do have the experience and the balls to tell you how to correct and overcome stuttering, my personal experience, my experience with thousands of people and my wisdom makes the other pass by, I'm very sorry if I show myself a bit egocentric but if you doubt any of the things I say, first think about who the hell is telling you. I also clarify something: many people come to be treated by speech therapists so that I can treat them, nothing happens with speech therapists, but let's see ... I mean ... or do you believe me that I have already gone through this and have helped thousands of people or you believe the "wise men".

Before starting with the reading exercises I will tell you what you will get. When you read, you are talking, many people who stutter make it difficult for them to read because as they speak they read, let me tell you that this is normal, it is normal, others read very well but they stutter when speaking, here this does not make sense, reading fluently and speaking stuttering does not It makes sense, if this happens it means that the improvement has much more weight, it is something more mental, it also does not mean that you do not make the correction, of course it does, it is just that you will have to give a lot of focus to the improvement because it is not logical that you speak fluently reading and that speaking you start to stutter, when I say that it is not logical I do not mean that it is weird, that is sooo common in the people who come to me, whether you stutter or not in the readings you will have to follow the same process .

The objective of the readings is to be able to master speech to the point that you mold it like clay.

Let's take any book, in this case I'm going to take an excerpt from my great friend Luis Miguel Morareu's book on Stuttering.

"I have been a hospice visitor at the Red Cross for two years, which can give you an idea of how many dying I have been able to see. I assure you that it is the people of this world who have taught me the most. Many of them, by way of conversation, related to me their lives and their exploits "

So, let's get started. There are several ways to read the text above (obviously) but what we are going to do and for you to understand me in the simplest way I will put it in a list below, do not worry if you do not understand, you will take the form.

1. Modulated reading
2. Paused Reading
3. Distorted Slow Reading
4. Interpretation Reading - Accents *
5. Read score changes.
6. Creative Readings

Here I mention the types of readings that you are going to have to do, these readings as I had said before is to release the language, flow and begin to couple the new linguistic structures. In short, you will become a master of language. This list that I mentioned is to make it constant, remember that everything is process, perseverance, daily life… and… and… and… do it big.

When you think about doing something, do not do it halfway, not for a short time, do it in a fun way in good weather, the people I treat I put an hour to two hours a day, after a short time they end up lengthening more to see their magnificent results, it is normal that you lengthen the time since you are getting on track.

They ask me which are the books that should be read. This of course is very subjective, but it is very easy to solve it, imagine that you are going to buy a meal, now think about what kind of food you will get the most out of. ho, any type of food that you choose at random or a type of food that you like :::: think about it :::: now that you thought about it it is obvious that you chose a type of food. It is the same with the readings, choose a type of reading that you like, be it drama, action, mystery, etc. What I tend to say to people is that they also choose some readings that I am going to contribute, for example: books on self-improvement, how to speak in public, books of teachings, advice, things that really contribute to you, remember that books are like friends: rare.

Like this I say is for you to take it sportingly, choose any book, reading or text, which it is: Hobligation with a capital "H" is to do it every day, every day, every day, every day, every day the days… in good weather, in good weather, in good weather, in good weather.

Remember that if one day you did not do it, you did not fail me, the truth sweats me, really. Many of the people I treated used to tell me that they had not been constant with the readings, and I would tell them: hey, you didn't fail me, you failed you, because you made a promise to yourself, just that. life will tell with your process of overcoming, if you give me things by halves, life will give you everything by halves too. This stuttering boy is very simple, do things, stop being stubborn and do what I tell you, then you will see the results and you will be able to speak or do whatever you want, meanwhile obey since someone who knows how tells you I know how to get over this.

Modulated reading.

Modulated reading is a reading where you are going to take the text and you will read it modulating each word, when I say modulating people open their mouths and modulate, that's fine but you need to get into the role boy, enjoy it. Read the text by opening your mouth in a subtle, interesting way, that you see that you open it and modulating each syllable as if you were residing the most beautiful poetry.

"Heeee siiiiii-doooo viiiii- siiiitador deeee…." Continuing with the previous text, it is reading by opening your mouth modulating each syllable you say and extending it.

Try to do the readings slowly, no one is chasing you. Many told me that they lived with people and how could they do it because they were suddenly deconcentrated. You have to remember that you have to give a damn what others think, but if it is at night and also people need rest or respect, you can do the readings without making a sound, that is, as if you were speaking without a voice, you will understand me, or when you whisper something that you don't want anyone to hear, you can do it that way too. Obviously it is better to do it with sound, but without sound it also works. What happens with these readings is that in the end you end up creating a new way of speaking, which some may like and others may not, that has to sweat you, the important thing is that at the end you feel comfortable with the way of speaking .

Paused Reading

This type of reading is very similar to the previous one, it is reading the text with pauses, for example:

"He (pause) si (pause) do (pause) vi (pause) si (pause) ta (pause) dor (pause) of pa-ci-en-tes ter-mi-na-les in the Cr-uz ro -You last two years… .. "

The idea is to put pauses in everything, practically read by syllables, one thing that is obvious but it does not need to be made clear is: this is an example, the idea is that you take a book and do sooooooo like that (what do you think? mamey) (many people only make a paragraph in this way, or a textico, that the truth is a recontramamada, it is useless, literally, do things right, learn this reflection: Everything you do no matter how diminutive it may be make it big, right and excellent)

Excellence is what defines the mediocre of the good, the mediocre are those who half-believe, those who half-do, those who half-try, the excellent are those who take and do everything macro, large, constant, with desire and energy, those are the ones that always come.

Slow reading

Slow Reading is also similar to the previous one, what changes is that in this one it will literally read as if you were a turtle reading, surely you have heard those distortions that sometimes make the music where it is placed Re-slow and the sound sounds. Very serious voice, as if it stopped in time, you will also do this type of reading, with the same form.

"Heeeeeeeeeeee   siiiiiiiiiiiiiiiidoooooooooooooooo   viiiiiiiiiiiisiiiiiiiiii-taaaaaaaaaaaaaaaaaadooooooooooooooooooooor   deeeeeeeeeeeeee paaaaaaaapatients…."

Make it slowooooo, if you saw how complex it is for people to pay attention (by God) to many people I told them to do this type of slow reading and what they did was read more slowly with a slow touch, look, here a touch does not work, a tad, a tris, here it serves slowoooooooooooooo lengthening the words to the maximum, until the paroxysm.

Interpretation reading *

This type of reading is the most important, that's right, I repeat, this way of reading. ra is the most fundamental, the most important, the TOP TOP, what will be up to you to correct it depends on this type of reading. Of course, you will have the intrigue of knowing why this type of reading. Let me explain, throughout my work with people I realized that this type of reading had the greatest effect, as well as in my personal life doing this type of reading was one of the pillars of my correction, indeed, as well as I read with this type of reading this is how I speak. Mmmm, could it be that you're already taking it, right?

This type of reading is the most valuable because here will be the new you, the way you read this reading is the way you will adopt when you talk to people. It's like saying a character change, as if you were someone else.

I want to make a clarification regarding the clown, as you well know Luismi is a great friend of mine, he talks about overcoming focused on the clown that is: doing the clown, has to do with disinhibiting yourself from everything by playing a role that is not you. You seem to me to be this form of improvement important, and adopting it is part of the process.

But ((as always the: but) I go more with the idea that you adopt a character but that deep down it is you, to see how I explain it to you, when you put on a mask and act like the character of that mask in The bottom line is you, I know that your personality varies and the way you speak but you are the one who plays the role. Having that clear is very important, because if not everything you are going to do with the readings will be something lost, since many people They tell me that they do not feel, that it matters that you do not feel, do not be like that, please, how ridiculous that, deep down you are obvious, remember what we talked about before, each role in our life we do with different mask, you do not behave the same with your partner as with your grandmother, we adopt multiple personalities, so putting yourself in the role of "another" so to speak opens many doors for you to find your best version, that's why I told you earlier than when I see myself years ago that is not me, now I am another role, now I am oy in another mask.

So when you start reading you will have to make multiple personalities, shapes, faces, whatever, the important thing is to find that you that makes you flow. When people do the clown, others are created and that is understandable, but to think that way is to give value to the character and that character does not have it, that is you, you are behind the backdrop, a movie does not look good for being film, behind the film there is someone who directs it, if it were not for the directors there would be no interesting film to tell, so give yourself the courage to know that you are the character.

All this stuff that I told you is so that later in the readings you do not start doubting things or asking nonsensical questions.

Now let's get started. When you read with this type of reading what you will do is a different character. For instance:

Role (hoarse older male voice)

"I have been a visitation of terminal patients in the Red Cross for two years, which can give you an idea of the number of dying that I have been able to see….

>>>>>>>>>>>>>>>>>>>>>>>> Read the above with that type of character <<<<<<<<<<<<<<<<<
Another role (super sassy young sexy woman voice)

"I have been a visitation of terminal patients in the Red Cross for two years, which can give you an idea of the number of dying that I have been able to see….

>>>>>>>>>>>>>>>>>>>>>>>> Read the above with that type of character <<<<<<<<<<<<<<<<<

Another role (infant toddler voice)

"I have been a visitation of terminal patients in the Red Cross for two years, which can give you an idea of the number of dying that I have been able to see….
>>>>>>>>>>>>>>>>>>>>>>>> Read the above with that type of character <<<<<<<<<<<<<<<<<
….
…………
…………….
Other papers
(Angry older woman's voice)
(Alpha male voice with skyrocketing self esteem)
(naughty restless girl voice)
……
… ..

… ..

Look for all the characters and try to do many readings with those types of characters that deep down you are playing a role of them. When you do all these characters, this is where you will have to find yours, your character or your best version, for example you do all these voices, then you are outlining yourself, if for example you are an insecure, shy boy and things like that, your last role The one you will always stay with is (the voice of a man with self-esteem through the roof) before having reached this point you will have to have gone through several such as (extroverted boy with high security) (boy believed with many friends)… ..etc ….etc…. They are examples ok! Now you have to create several characters and profile them.

Something that I used to use with people was that in a book every two paragraphs they change character or every three paragraphs, so that the reading does not become monotonous or you get bored but so that there are those changes of turn, those evolutions, what What happened was greater effect since a lot is played with speech.
This will clearly make you become a master of language (literal) Remember that the goal is that the role that you are going to outline will be your own role in life, the way you adopt in the readings is the way you will end up speaking, This is something that happens naturally with the process, it is not something that you have to impose, that is happening for the same as always, for carrying a constant process, so do not worry if you are not finding the character or you do not feel that you are. leading to real life so to speak, that will just happen.

Interpretive Reading

This reading, the same as the previous one, means this:

After overcoming my stuttering I wanted to enter a theater academy, I really learned many things, something that I remember a lot was when the teacher put us to read in class. When we were all reading he stood in front of one of my classmates and said: Don't read me. My colleague, confused by not understanding, told him: you told me to read. My teacher told him again: -do not read, interpret- We are all like What the hell? "Interpret" something that my teacher took a silence and said:

Most people when they are asked to read or when they read by themselves what they do is spit out nonsense words, when you go to read interpret with passion (at that moment the teacher puts his hand to his stomach and says: from here is where he has to say things) when you perform you enjoy it, you do it with energy, and besides that ... you make a show for others.

All those days we agreed with him, and after that we never read again, we always interpreted the words we said as if we were living in our own flesh.

That is why I invite you in this type of reading, to live each word, to eat the story, to really interpret what you read, because if you saw the number of people who came to read me, I would teach them to interpret and they came back again and read, it is as if there was a wall between normal and excellent, that is why excellence is much higher, it is not that normal and excellent have an extra as they say, in truth it is a long way to go. reach excellence, although more than a stretch is desire, that you really take the advice and apply it.

Every word you read live it, gesticulate too. There are people who speak without any expression, what the hell is that? Express yourself, why are you going to save your emotions? People keep feelings for after they are dead, I think. Certain people tell me that if it is good to move when you speak, gesture, wink, accents, I tell them that all that is excellent, it is great to give an orchestra to your speech, that you enjoy it, that you have a good time, that is Like a symphony where everything communicates, for that you were given all the tools you have, take advantage of it, the best coaches are the ones who get all the emotion, the ones who keep quiet and stay there without saying anything or expressing 0 emotions, then they leave coming out. People want desire, spark, energy, vibrate with that, the difference between arriving or not arriving is ATTITUDE. Example of correction and overcoming of stuttering
"This is the key point of this book"

Attention!! Pay close attention to this part because it collects everything you will have to do in correcting and overcoming stuttering, I could have done a step by step as a principles style: Rule 1, Rule 2, Rule 3 ... etc ... etc ... or also do this, then this, then that, and just like serially, and that's okay! It could be done like this, although I think there is nothing better than an example that has all that together, and that you, through the example, can apply everything that is said. Nothing is as important as learning by example, because with the real example you can see in detail, the step by step as it is.

I will explain to you how is the whole stage of Overcoming and Correcting Stuttering, everything very to the millimeter, I am going to narrate it through a story in which you are going to get there in the film, the idea is that this story is become your story, which as you read it you get into character.

Before I start, I have to tell you that all those who overcome and correct stuttering go through this same story, some things change or are done in disorder, but the step-by-step path is always the same. Here I also do not detail things that are not worth it, such as adopting a personality type, or how old you should be or that you have to have such a shape or get this or that, not at all, that's shit and it doesn't matter. Here I will tell you the punctual, the concrete, the most important, bluntly, if you do not see something here it is because it does not matter so much, or literally it does not matter, or it could have been clear to me, although if it happens to me it does not matter, I never know the most important obvious thing would happen to me.

We are going to talk about the case of Pedro, in this case Pedro will be you. Remember again: Pedro is you, this is for you to go mentally.

Pedro is a boy who has a stutter, who has not overcome it or corrected it. Pedro is divided into two phases (let's call it phases, divisions, factors, components...) In one it is the Mental part and in the Other it is the Physical Phase.

-------------------------   Mental   Part   --------------------

-----------------Physical part-------------------

These two components when they come together is what makes Peter so to speak.

In the Mental component are beliefs, what Peter says, what he thinks, what he idealizes, all that is there, it is what we call the Ego or the pixie. Pedro in this component thinks the following:

• My stuttering is bad
• Stuttering is Horrible
• I don't know why I have this
• It is a disease
• This is a problem
• What will be of my life
• Why don't I get out of here
• Why me
• It's the worst thing he could have given me
• Stuttering limits me
• I reject stuttering completely
• I am different from others because others speak fluently
• Etc…

Pedro has a series of constant thoughts that he reinforces with more thoughts which makes him have a critical mindset.

In the physical component is speech, voice, language, the speech apparatus, everything that is tangible, what we call hardware. Pedro has the following:

• Pedro's words stick
• he has blocks when he speaks
• he has trouble breathing
• It gets stuck in every sentence
• The letters m, c, p cost a lot
• he has words where he replaces them because he can't get them out
• When he speaks he is breathless and his veins swell

- he turns red when he speaks, his throat tightens
- His mouth cords seem tangled
- Pedro, no matter how much he does to
him, does not get a few words out
- Etc…

Pedro has the idea that he always arrives at the same thing, that there is no escape, everything that he seeks, does, investigates leads him to …… the same, that: the same.

Why? Because Pedro is a boy who uses the same belief system day after day, month after month, year after year, he doesn't realize that really thinking like this will not get him anywhere, it will always be …… THE SAME… exact: THE SAME.

Pedro, day after day, denies stuttering, rejects it, thinks the same, that's why he has the same results. This boy does not understand that to have different results you have to think differently, if only Pedro knew this phrase and instilled it well, his life would change.

It is crazy to have different results by always thinking and doing the same thing.

But that doesn't happen, Pedro is still the same, why? Because deep down deep down Pedro doesn't want to overcome stuttering, it's hard for this boy to think that, but it's the truth, he feels comfortable there, he likes to reject himself, he likes to criticize stuttering, he loves to hide, he loves to think Every day that will become of his life, the many limitations that he has with stuttering, all that amazes Pedro, of course he thinks not, obviously, he thinks it is not like that. If you asked Pedro if he loves to be like that, he would tell you that he wouldn't even think that in curves, but deep down where he can't access because he hasn't realized that he feels very comfortable like that, of what he does.
he would not go on doing the same thing.

What Pedro has to do is realize, it is the first magic word, it sounds even beautiful to say it: "Realize" have you ever realized that that path was not, or that the decision you were making was wrong, it feels like a peace, you were so lost that when you realized it you said: wow! Now yes!

Pedro has to realize that thinking with that same system of thought will lead him to think the same, that is, to nothing, what he thinks tomorrow, in a few days, in a month, the things he does, the results, the actions, will they take you to? the same is so why? because the belief system is always replicated.

Note: it must be said that at this stage it is difficult to understand it well, well, it is not difficult, we make it so complex, because as we already have charcoal-roasted beliefs, thinking that there are better ones or that what I think is wrong is complex , I know, I know, but you will have to see that it could be that what you think is false.

Pedro rejects the other ideas, he hides himself thinking that since he thinks it is right, he does not open himself to the possibility that his beliefs are wrong. Pedro continues on his way and will do the following.

1) Peter will become a Seeker: he will sneak into his own thoughts, find a way to give more weight to what he thinks and forcefully reject what does not go with his thoughts. He will start looking for things about stuttering, information, research, everything that is related to what he thinks, if something comes out that does not go in his position, he rejects it, indeed, does not look at it. Pedro will become a great seeker of what he thinks is right.

Note: this is a typical path where people stay looking and become a "seeker" who searches, searches, searches and keeps looking ... looking for nothing because it is always the same circle, hence the phrase: always came to the same, you can not find a solution, give me a cure, what is the formula, etc ...

2) Peter will become a Questioner: on this path, Peter will ask himself what we said earlier: Why do I have a stutter? Where did your stuttering come from? What was the trigger? How did everything happen?

Thinking that at some point knowing the answer can lead to the solution (obviously it will not happen in this life or in the next)

3) Pedro will become a Cursomano: As Pedro he has nowhere to go and his belief system is old and leads him to the same thing, anything will make him move the floor, or anyone will whistle little birds in the air. Pedro will begin to do courses, workshops, programs, therapies, treatments, hypnosis, healings and any other blowjob that he has out there to stop stuttering.

Note: All these things about therapies, courses, treatments, what they do is reinforce more the belief system that Pedro has because the base from which all these things are done is rejection, it is: -We are going to heal you but deep down we want that you stop stuttering, that's why we heal you - / -We will do hypnosis so that you stop stuttering at once, that is what hypnosis is for so that you enter a trance from which you let go of stuttering- (as if the mind were stuttering and said : you are giving me a super-ultra-powerful hypnosis, I will stop stuttering right away) Look, the initiative with what you do something determines if you will reach the same with warm water cloths or if you will really change (another thing would be if the initiative that you start these things is to experience that there it would be different)

4) Pedro will become a Swimmer: Here at this point Pedro will simply do absolutely nothing, no liner, nothing at all. Pedro will say: you know that ... the truth is I will not do anything to change my life, I will stay the same, just as it is.

These are the 4 paths that Pedro can take and stay there for years and years, they are not bad paths, indeed, one should go through all those paths to find the truth, it is not necessary to go through all that or stay a century there, it is important to see yourself, analyze yourself, in a few words: Realize.

Suppose now that Peter realizes after this, now Peter realizes that continuing in the same way is a waste of life. Pedro, the first thing he will do is look for new information or content that goes against what he thinks. Why? because he knows that his belief system is wrong, or maybe he could be wrong. Pedro begins to feel things are judging him, new perspectives, other points of view, he opens up to look at new concepts, different thoughts, scrutinizes about the new knowledge without saying that it is lies or truth, he simply looks at it.

When Pedro analyzes, looks, searches, feels the content he will realize that the end goal of stuttering is acceptance, which goes against his belief system, but is the only way out. If the belief system is based on the rejection of stuttering, the con would be to accept stuttering.

Pedro then begins to see content like this book, to read the myths of stuttering, to think that everything they had been told is false, to look at more content that talks about the issues that I commented, to go for that different position, a position of improvement, self-help, inspiration, of motivation, of mental change.

Pedro eats everything I have said in the book, although it is rare, but it can happen, it has happened with few people, and it is that Pedro ends up doubting and returns, aiiishhhh that fails, he returns, wait! It is not a failure, it is normal, because if you think about letting go of one belief system for another requires a process, which Pedro has not had and is at the stage where he doubts that it is an excellent stage, why? because he already doubts it, he doubts that it could be that what he thinks is false.

Pedro then goes back to the old belief system that is greater than the new belief system, the old system is more consolidated, firmer, to think that a new belief system will replace the old one that suddenly is rare, it can happen, but it is process. The beauty of this, both of returning and not returning is that Pedro has already begun the stage of overcoming without realizing it (hahahahaha this is crazy but it is reality) Pedro has already opened up to that knowledge of the new belief system because he already knows He implanted that seed in him, so even if Peter is in the old belief system, he will want to keep trying the new belief system.

Note: it is the same thing that happens with the people I deal with, they come to me, I tell them the path of stuttering, they doubt it, then they stay where they were before and after a few days they come back to me again to continue with the process ... (That part is funny, it always makes me laugh when they keep their posture so firm and then they break back again as if they had been ringing something... .that... .the thing that remains ringing is the seed that has been implanted) This is like when you try something you like and people say you can't do it so you reserve it, but you liked it so much that then you try again and stay at it, your thoughts will do their best to stay away but once you try not there is going back why? because you are so tired of hanging around in the same thing that it makes you play it "the last card is many times the one you least thought it was"

Pedro comes back this time with the idea that it could be, suddenly, maybe ... I could try, his belief system changes from not believing to trying and the first phase of Pedro begins.

"Realize really" Pedro now if he realizes, the above was an assumption, now if Pedro definitely says: "Damn, I was thinking very badly" Pedro opens up to new knowledge. In this journey of Pedro feeding on new content such as the myths of stutterers, the acceptance, the approval of others, all those concepts Pedro swallows them with chips and salsa, so to speak.

Note: on this path Pedro injects everything I say in the book, he believes it, he puts it in his brain, it's the same thing you should do, that's why I save myself all that step that Pedro will do with knowledge because you already have it in the book.

Note: another little thing that I forgot and that I don't know if I said in the book: In order for you to capture what a content really says, you have to read it at least three times. When people read people only read without learning, when they read for the second time they draw the conclusion of what they believe, when they read for the third time they draw the conclusion of what the reader really wants to say. It is important that you read and reread this book.

Let's continue with Pedro. Along the way when he adapts all these concepts he will meet the thoughts on several occasions that will tell him phrases such as:

• It will be very difficult, leave it
• It is more of the same
• We are giving back
• That will take a long time
• Accepting yourself seems silly to me
• Accepting yourself… it can't be that simple
• All this I feel more emotional
• I want something more technical
• I feel more comfortable where I was

The old belief system is more comfortable and therefore thoughts will always come that will pull you, it is like because if it was not comfortable Pedro would not have created it, pay attention to this, if his old belief system had not been comfortable Pedro would have left a long time ago from there to create another belief system, that's why when I say that people like to be there it is true, if you do not believe, well there you, but in my experience with many people it is like that, hey and not only with stutterers, with all.

Note: It does not mean that Pedro is happy, eye! I've never said that, Pedro suffers because the thought of him leads him nowhere, that's why people come to me suffering because they see no way out.

There will be many cases where Pedro questions himself thinking that this path of acceptance is lies, that he does not believe, that he does not know, and that he can invent. At this point Pedro could return as many times as he wanted, this is where the speed is divided, the one with the fastest 1 A surpasses is the one that comes out of that circle, the one that surpasses it slower is the one that stays spinning, but in the end it manages to come out, as I said before, no matter how long it takes, the important thing is to keep going.

Once the seed is put in, it is rare to remove that, what I will tell you is important to emphasize it again: You will feel that you return many times, as it has no way out, but it is because of the struggle of old and new beliefs, calm down and continue , you never turn back, you are always moving forward. When I talk about Pedro returning, he does not really return, he returns to contrast one thing with another, to clean up those old beliefs that whisper to him, these delays are normal, it is very normal. I like to make an analogy with the arrow, when you launch the arrow there are many factors that make the arrow lose speed and it seems that it will not hit the target, in the end it hits the target because the arrow has more focus than what can surround you. You are the arrow that despite distractions or external factors do not lose sight of the goal (Remember the vision)

Again let's go back to Pedro, after so many jerks he enters the path of Acceptance or what is called the Change of Thought. It changes from an approach of rejection where I do not want the stuttering, I reject it, I want to remove it, eliminate it, remove this from my life, be different, for a change of acceptance.

Here Pedro begins the path of Overcoming. Every day Pedro begins to look for new readings of rational psychology, he begins to speak with people to help them or to start conversations from the constructive point of view, he looks for information that goes according to that new thought, he talks to teachers of this approach, he is going to look at all this, he enters this world, he already loves everything about it, but here something curious begins….

After so much, Pedro can take that initiative of acceptance or stay stuck there for a reason that I will explain to you again. Pedro once in the world of overcoming can go like smooth sailing, but he may not and the reason why he is not because of the cost X benefit. You remember? The vision.

Pedro can focus more on the effort it will take instead of how great it can be, so consuming the content, doing the actions, researching the topic, reading books, among other things, can be seen as expensive.

Note: Remember that the difference between sticking with the process and not sticking with it is a matter of focus, or you focus on profit or effort. You always have to focus on how great it can be to overcome stuttering, otherwise you will see it complex. Focused on profit you know where you will go. If you go to the gym and concentrate on everything you have to do every day to reach huge muscles, it will hit you very hard, you probably won't get there, but if you envision what you can achieve when you do the whole process or if you envision yourself How you will be, how great you are going to look, the body and health change that you are going to have with the effort will become minimal.

What Pedro has to do is be very clear about the vision that we explained in great detail above (this point is very important)

Pedro then when he has a clear vision, he is looking at content, feeding his mind with a new belief system and all that. Then what he will have to do is argue daily about the new beliefs or the new thought system. Why is it better to let go of the approval of others, because it is better to have high self-esteem, because it is better to accept yourself, because it is better to screw others, because it is better to take responsibility for yourself, because stuttering is good, because stuttering has come into his life, because it has given him the possibility to see himself, to transform himself, to be different. It should be filled with strong thoughts, affirmations, inspiring music, examples of overcoming, motivated ... etc ... etc ... etc ... constantly during the day, weeks, months, everything that is contrary to how I thought before should be argued.

Pedro literally injects what is said in this book about acceptance, self-esteem and the approval of others.

Then when Peter has all these things in which every day he has argued he will find a mountain. Let's imagine Pedro with his big head full of all this new content, arguments, affirmations, his head is in the TOP-TOP in front of this a very high mountain which needs to reach the top, to this route from where Pedro is to the top of the mountain are the actions or "taking action" this is where you have to take action.

Note: This point is key because you can already see the mountain, you know what to do and the only thing left to do is to climb it, but here many are left in doubt because they think that the actions can do more or are justified by thinking that the actions do not have the weight enough or it won't get them out of stuttering (which is ridiculous with all that they say because how do people start the actions they stay doing them since they see the results) at this point you will have to be strong, capable, have tenacity, when the waves carry you you will have to continue, remember that there is no step but you climb the mountain, there is no other than doing the actions.

Then Peter will think two things or he does it or he doesn't and he does. If Pedro takes action it means that his thoughts have led him to take action, that means that everything that he has in his head has given him the plus to make that decision. If Pedro does not take action, it means that he needs to reinforce those thoughts, he needs to give them more weight, to inflate that head more so to speak. A phrase says I don't know if I repeated it up there, which is: "You take action when your mind has decided to take action" (As this phrase says, that's the way it is, that's why many stand still at this point, wait, wait, wait, until your mind makes up its mind, if you don't decide you need to reinforce the mind more)

Pedro takes action peeeerooo here he must be attentive to something: to what?: "To his expectations" because although it is important to have a clear vision, it is important not to have expectations of the path that you will find. Suppose that Pedro begins to climb the mountain with the idea that it will be a clean path, without obstacles, without potholes along the way and he gets the idea that by taking action he is ready, but... on the way that does not happen, he finds bushes, roads that lead elsewhere, hunting animals, unfavorable weather, and many factors that can make Pedro frustrated because his expectations do not match reality.

The same thing can happen, that you go with the expectation that you will do some amazing actions and all that, let me tell you that that does not happen, especially at the beginning, when you do the actions you may not feel good, that things go wrong. That you do not find a connection, that you do not want to continue, many things can happen, but if you stay firm you will achieve it, if your expectations of actions were like sweet lemons that is a great lie. Expectations of the road are useless, stay in the vision with 0 expectations of the road. There is a myth in stuttering to think that stuttering is overcome or corrected by taking large steps, I clarify that stuttering in most cases or in all is overcome with small steps, what I call steps.

To climb the mountain you will not climb it like crazy, or by racing since you can sink and become stagnant. What Pedro has to do is climb in small steps. Pedro cannot start to go out and call everyone, that is ridiculous, the first thing he has to do is do an action that he feels good but that he has not done, this may sound strange but I give an example: in my life I had never gone out with clothes backwards, but I feel comfortable doing it, I would not have any fear, so I do it, if I have any fear I will leave it for later (be careful, here it is important to get out of the comfort zone a little, that's why I said : do things that Pedro has not done) (I open parentheses again, remember that you always have to leave the area, attentive to the phrase that says: "Success is on the other side of fear" and the phrase: "If you want to have different results you will have to do different things "

Pedro then considers one of the steps and it is: call everyone on the phone, although he analyzes this action well and thinks that it is a lot, that it will be complex for him and decides to shorten it more and take that action that looks great In small steps that can be: calling unknown people, or calling only three people or one, that depends on Pedro and as far as he can loosen.

Pedro then decides the action of calling three people, and not talking to them but saying hello and hanging up because he still does not feel comfortable "but" this action had never been performed (that is the important thing)

Note: There is something that happened to me, obviously everyone is different, I was terrified of the telephone, I never started with those actions of the telephone, I started going out on the street because it was more comfortable for me to start from there since the People did not know me and I could get more out of it there, so I started to greet people, then I did more things and so on, and around when I became very confident I started doing actions on the phone.

Pedro climbs step by step, the ideal is for Pedro to do it day by day, is it the ideal? -----> NO, it is MANDATORY !!!!!!!!!!! That is why overcoming stuttering in a month is sooooo possible, imagine being in that tune every day, you will become a monster.

Note: I am sorry for so many notes, there are little things that are going to happen to you and it is important that you have it very yyy clear. On the road there will be bumps as I said before, there will be things that play against, it is your ability to move forward that determines the time it will take you to move forward, achieving it or not depends a lot on whether you remain constant despite those falls. why? because the falls are very normalll -----> too normal. It is normal to feel a delay in the actions and at the same time feel that you are returning, because as you buy one action with another you think that yesterday you were better, but that is lies, your mind plays tricks on you, it is also normal to think about the negative, But do not focus on that, negative things are normal, we are human beings and we focus on errors for a matter of evolution, do not focus on that now, that is no longer useful, errors are very normal, there are days where you will do some comfortable actions with good results and there are others where you will not, that does not really matter, the important thing is to continue, many guys have been telling me that they had done, for example, an action of going to the commercial premises and shouting and they told me that this This action had been excellent for this and this, I told them: -Don't focus on the result, focus on doing things- then a few days later they came frustrated because they had done the same action but this time they did not see good results or they told me n silly things about results, and I once again told them: - not to focus on the result since there comes a point where you do so many actions that the result is worth a three. It is normal to think about the result when you have little experience in something, it is something natural.

I do not know if you knew that when someone studies any subject and studies a good short time, they already believe that they know a lot about it, but in reality they do not know much, they know little, that happens, it is something scientific, it is the same with this, Do you think that by doing two or three actions you put yourself in the clouds or start to draw conclusions, nah, nah, nah, that is nothing to stay there, when you do many actions you will see that the result is spent with toilet paper, because now you focus on doing and doing more, and the results come alone, alone, why? because you have already done so many actions that you acquire a fortress that you shit, you become a monster and that is the peak.

Remember that life has more ups than downs, this life is like a canvas where some black spots are bumps, when you look at the complete painting the bumps are not visible, why? because potholes are so much less than the beautiful things in life.

Anecdote:
I like to tell an anecdote about how I learned to swim. I was terrified of swimming, why? I really have no idea, something I could remember is that my dad was afraid of water and when he saw him he could see that he was afraid of him. When I was little, I was admitted to swimming classes and the truth is that the moments when I was in those classes I became more afraid of him, since many boys crowded on top of me or jumped and all this scared me. I remember that when I was in class a classmate I knew from school was also there and I remember how she threw herself on my back and I immediately sank, I came out of the water like a beast to breathe and wow that moment was crazy for me, I was angry with my partner, I left the classes, and sent everything to hell.

After the moments with the pool it was to swallow water, until once a little bigger I saw the movie the ice age. There is a part where "Sid" (the lazy bear) teaches "Diego" (saber tooth tiger) to swim and tells him that swimming is very easy that he only has to do kick-arm, kick-arm, kick-arm , Diego after this still felt fear. In one part of the movie everything collapses and the tiger (Diego) has to jump into the water, so he jumps into the water and remembers what Sid had told him and starts swimming. When I saw that piece of the movie I said: Wow! It shouldn't be so complicated to swim, it's arm-kick and so on, then I started to see more videos of how children swim and even when they throw a baby into the water like this one begins to swim.

I remember that I went to the sea with my parents and the sea seemed different to me, and the water seemed manageable. My dad used to carry a ball and hold onto it to put his head in, I couldn't do that, I was still scared, until I saw that he did it with such ease that I decided to do it too and boy did I do it! I was able to swim with the ball and put my head in, I remembered what I saw in the ice age movie and started running the water with my hands and kicking, I did this consecutively and wow! It was keeping me in the water! In my mind I remember thinking: if I fall or something happens, or I sink then I just stop and that's it, I don't have to be afraid because if something happens I just stop because I am higher than the water level.

One day I went to a farm with my parents and the pool was alone, my mom got into the pool and started swimming and so did my brother, my dad always stayed on the shore, me too hahaha but I already felt the water different, With everything she had seen and that time at sea she felt that the water could control her. I watched as my mother swam relaxed and easy through the water. She came to a point where she told me that if she wanted to learn to swim and I told her Yes, he told me to learn to swim with the head out before, and all of us who have gone through a stage to learn to swim know that putting your head in is very difficult when you are afraid of water, so my mother taught me to swim sideways, sideways? That was ridiculous but I started to swim sideways kicking and stroking and keeping my head out of the water, I also thought that if I fell, or sank, or did not hit, I would stand up and that's it, because it was higher than the water level. water, that kept me a little safe.

This is how little by little I began to swim, to take away the fear of water, after a short time I went back to swimming lessons, I also competed in swimming races, I went many times to the pool to swim and the water had stopped being a monster and it had become one of the things I enjoyed the most in its time.

I wanted to swim everything, every time I got into the water I felt more and more security in myself, I got to the point of doing everything swimmers do such as laps, dives, rolls, all kinds of acrobatics in the water, it was practically a dolphin hahahaha.

You know ... the same applies in many aspects of life, when you want to overcome something you study it, you understand it, you look at new perspectives, you start to get into the mud and you gradually remove the fear of that which disturbs you.

If I had known the key to removing the fear of water I would have done it a long time ago, but people do not tell you because they do not know, they only think that fear is something natural that only by jumping into the water you can overcome it, and that is lies, my friend .

Today a child learns to swim in a simple way, first he is taught that water is a means to enjoy, to have a good time, that it is not that typical Monster in which you drown, or that if you slip you stay there and the water will do its best to sink you. The boy later is taught how to get into the water, if he is afraid he only enters his feet and slowly details the water, after a few days he gets into the water but walking, he understands it, touches it, walks and walks, the other days move his hands, feet, and go little by little, then he just sticks his head in and takes it out, puts it in and takes it out, and so step by step the child sees that water is something natural and every time he does these actions he is acquiring self-assurance.

If the child is thrown into the water to learn to swim, he may become more afraid because that monster can turn into a thousand demons that all it does is disturb him for the rest of his life, or he may learn to swim of course, which is also not that beneficial since there is nothing like doing things with a process in a way that is enjoyable, how can you enjoy being thrown into the water knowing that you are afraid? That is not a good way.

Anecdote of the mountaineers:

There is an anecdote about mountaineers that I tell many times and that is that most people think that mountaineers are people who climb the mountain like that and that is not true, the mountaineers first what they do is study the mountain they climbed, the they analyze, they look at strategies for easy access. Once they start to climb they create what is known as base camps, base camps with small shelters where they spend the night to continue climbing the next day. The interesting thing is that as they advance they leave base camps, if for example they are climbing and feel that the conditions are not favorable or one of their companions has problems, they return to the camp they left behind, and the next day they wait to return to upload. (That is why it is important to stay safe, I advance but I can give back a little if I see that it is still not enough or it is not the moment or I lack some more actions to go back up) They do not say: we are going to climb the mountain and give it -dele-le and go up and up and up and we have to take risks with everything, NOOOOO, that's ridiculous, what's more, when the mountaineers go up that way many of them die because they are not trained or their body does not finish adapting to the conditions. Everything has a process, the body as well as the mind needs to establish itself, take control, gain confidence, acclimatise, get in tune first to be able to climb little by little, that myth of taking risks and breaking it is lies, it is pure publicity, or those who They say: Do it !!! You can!!! Go and take a chance !!! Noo that is silly, you think that if you say that to someone who is afraid of something all his life, he will launch himself just like that, nooo, that will not happen, because the human being is a being of process, of learning and that person has learned to be afraid of that something and that is very normal, the only way to leave it is by relearning and starting over step by step ... ... remember: everything in this life is PROCESS.

Don't see setbacks as setbacks but rather as enhancers ...

Continuing with Pedro:

Pedro has already reached the top with the actions and the process. Pedro realizes here something: he realizes that he is now free, but free of it, it is very reminiscent of the caveman story.

The cave man:

A man lived in a prison hidden in a dark cavern, every day he went out to look for something to eat. One day the man lost the keys to the jail where he was locked up every day, very worried he went looking for the key everywhere but did not find it, he constantly left the caverns asking people where the key was, people without having The idea was getting away from him, the years went by and the man kept looking for the key without finding it. Before he died, a monk passed by him and the man said to him: -Sir, have you seen where I left the key? The monk, thinking, said to him: Have you already looked in your pockets? The man replied: why would I search my pockets? The monk tells him: -because that's the last place you would look- The man, putting his hands in his pockets, realizes that he has the key, he is very surprised by this and says: -Well, I don't believe it! He soon realizes that there is an engraving on the key that says: "This key was made by me", he immediately runs to the jail and on the jail plate there is another engraving that says: "and this jail too" It happens with stuttering, we are the creators of that whole world that we tell ourselves, I don't know why some people make stuttering a global, complex thing, something super stormy, in the end you are the one who creates that storm, for me not It is a storm, now of course, before it was, because now I design my life, there is the difference, that is what you will end up doing, designing your own life realizing the prison that you have created)

After Pedro recalls this story, he realizes that it is not enough just to overcome, if it is beautiful, cool, but the important thing after over-coming is to help others to overcome as well, because that cycle must be closed, when you are helped by someone you close a cycle when you help another or more people, since you learn twice as much, and you also understand that this is the true path.

Pedro then decides to contact people with stuttering to help them on their path of improvement, providing them with all the knowledge in this book and keeping a close eye on the person to guide them on the best path.

After having overcome stuttering, Pedro decides if he wants to correct it (at this point you decide, something I have to tell you is that many of those who overcome stuttering correct it at the same time and others when they overcome it start the path of correction, others few feel good without correcting it and they stay that way)

Pedro then decides to correct the stuttering and begins with the readings. Pedro loves self-help books a lot, because he knows that in addition to practicing speaking he can also learn, "it's like killing two birds with one stone" so he starts reading books, Pedro starts to take that as a habit and not as " a reading patch "a plan is proposed, in 30 days he will read an average of 2 hours a day that will increase in some days, he is so determined to correct stuttering that in some days he considers reading more than 5 hours! Because he knows that the more he reads, the more he will develop his linguistic part of speech.

Pedro applies daily the types of reading that are proposed in this book such as interpretive reading, reading with pauses, reading with characters, and all kinds of readings to master speaking with his hands, Pedro decides to implement a plan.

(A Plan is what allows you to connect a point "A" to a point "B", in this case it would be from where you start to where you end, in a few words it is to put fire to the pot so that it does not remain astonished, if you want that the results have progress you will have to design a daily plan like the following one that Pedro will do)

Day 1: Pedro gets up in the morning and visualizes what he wants to become. Pedro also visualizes the day in a constructive way, for example: when work arrives I will speak calmly with my colleagues, I will show my best face, I will not give a damn what they think and I will make a few talks. Pedro in the course of the day will think why stuttering is good and he will argue about all those things, Pedro thinks that it is best to use a handle or badge that always reminds him of arguing since he is a bit forgetful.

-Then during the day he argues in every situation: why accepting yourself is the best there is.

-On this first day Pedro decides to do the action of going to work with his jacket inside out.

-Also on this first day another of the actions that Pedro does is pick up the phone and talk as if he were talking to someone.

Note: I did this action many times, to take out the phone and speak as if there were another person on the other line, I did not call anyone, I simply spoke on the phone, because when you talk on the phone, many people listen and that takes me out. a lot of the comfort zone, because I felt that everyone listens to me and that gave me more security, I always tell people that doing these actions is like carrying a backpack full of actions, the more you load yourself the more you are prepared for whatever it is, when a situation comes you know how to handle it very good (I consider this action to be very important, one of the most important, because you do two for one, you talk and besides that people hear you and you start to be very creative holding a conversation (pretend you were talking on the phone, I say this if suddenly you have not understood this action)

-That same day Pedro decides to do character reading for 2 hours.

- During the night Pedro reflects on what happened in the day, if there were events where he felt less than the others he reflects on them and changes that way of thinking, if he gave approval, he reflects on it and is about to transform that idea, that's how it goes seeing one by one all the events of the day and one by one he transforms them in a CONSTRUCTIVE-POSITIVE way.

-Pedro before going to sleep visualizes himself, listens to affirmations, writes down powerful words and sees motivating content.

Day 2: Pedro gets up in the morning and does the same as the day before
...

Day 3: Pedro gets up in the morning and does the same as the day before....

Day 4: Pedro gets up in the morning and does the same thing as the day before, although this time he decides to put a touch of fire in the action.

-Pedro decides to do an action to call two relatives and greet them nothing more.

-Pedro that same day decides to read for 4 hours doing paused reading with breathing and jumping reading.

-Day 5: Pedro gets up in the morning and does the same as every previous day, but this time he decides to go out and have a conversation with people.

-Pedro feels that he has not done well, so he does not worry because he knows that the important thing is the process, so he decides to return a little to the actions of greeting his relatives and try to do it more times to regain self-esteem.

Day 7,8,9,10: Pedro does the same as the previous days and raises the level of the shares.

Day 11: Pedro goes out into the street to hold conversations.

-Pedro reads like the gods and decides to read 6 more hours to increase the correction.

-Pedro also decides to increase the actions by doing 7 actions a day. (He remembers that the more actions Pedro makes, the more confidence he takes and in turn, the more experience he acquires)

Day 12,13,14: Pedro does the same as the previous days and decides to increase the actions because they know that the actions are a gold medal, the rest is a silver medal and the rest a bronze medal (remember this very well)

Day 15,16,17,18: Pedro decides to set fire to the actions. He goes out into the streets and shouts, reads in public, does everything to make people look at him, what they call ridiculous is the plus for Pedro to gain more security.

-Pedro calls Reymundo and everyone, reserves rooms to cancel, asks for addresses to cancel, calls people to talk to them about another religion or sensitive topics, because he knows that what others think has to matter a three to him.

-Pedro in the new actions decides many times to go against what people want or think to gain security, confidence and self-esteem.

Day 19,20,21: Pedro continues with the shares increasing the volume every day.

-Although Pedro in some actions feels that he returns, he compensates it with more actions, he is a true machine.

Day 22,23,24: Pedro these days if he has done the above very well and consistently without skipping any step or process, he will be like the gods: in the clouds.

-Pedro sometimes thinks of skipping some actions because he believes that he has already done them or that he has an easy time, then remember that the most important are the steps but not the jumps, because the jumps, even if they look large, do not keep a gradual constancy that you It gives hardness (this is like a column, for a column to be resistant you have to be patient, use good concrete and wait for it to dry, if you skip the columns the house will fall) (literal)

Days 25,26,27,28,28,30: Pedro in these stages is very likely to begin to notice the overcoming of stuttering, because he has realized that this is the true path of overcoming, when you realize you have already surpassed him.

-Pedro begins to enjoy the process

-When Pedro enjoys the process this makes it everyday.

Day 31 and others: Pedro will continue doing all this until he acquires more strength, and then he will see if he does some things, if he no longer does, or so (they ask me if I still do this, I honestly do it from time to time, but I do it because I like it, because I have a good time, I still do the affirmations, and some other actions, these things that recharge me, it's like a dose) one day I heard someone say: how long do I have to make affirmations? I told him: all your life, if you feed your body every day, why don't you feed your mind every day?

If I don't keep doing these things, it's like I'm I will be short of breath, this keeps me on top, great minds never stop studying, because you think about stopping, if something suits you, follow it, make it a habit, never stop doing it, that will keep you much higher.

Analyze something: if all your life you have built a system of thought that does not work, why not make this new system of thought and that it is good for you all your life?

My Overcoming Story:

Real anecdote of my life

And to close with a flourish because my life story was missing, which I have called my personal improvement. As a child, like many close to me, they know that I had a stutter all my life, practically since I can remember and I knew I had something. As a child you don't know that you stutter: obviously, although now it's easier for the little ones to explain them, but before there was no internet like today, my childhood was different, you played in the street with friends, with dolls, and things like that.

I do not want to say like many other people that childhood before was better or was more fun, mmmm that is very relative, each one takes the side that suits them, now children may say that they had the best childhood and that they other children from another era were stone picks.

In my childhood I did not have access to the internet, I did not know what I had and people only told me that it was "gago" something that the truth I never understood until after I grew up. I remember in school that many classmates approached me as well as other children from other grades and told me to say such phrases as: -I bathe every day- -My mother cooks very well- I repeated them and among everyone they laughed and They said: Ohhh this is it! This is! This is the one who gags and they all said: WOW how strange, how curious that is, he eats a lot of salt - hey do you eat a lot of salt? - They told me, I really did not understand this very well, I did not understand the salt, it is so much that when I was growing up I ate sugar because the salt had me up to the balls with that, it is curious because on many occasions they challenged me to say many phrases for them to laugh, I did my best to say it well but he hit me in many words, I thought a lot, why is this happening to me?

When I was growing up, the teachers talked with my mother about how the speech therapy was going since my parents took me to several speech therapists, but the face of speech therapists when they treated me suggested that it was difficult for me to stop stuttering.

I remember many visits to the speech therapist, talks with teachers, family members, everything about stuttering, but the truth is that I did not understand practically anything, it was more my parents' concern than mine, all I wanted was to play, have fun, those Situations frustrated me a lot, if I remember many sad moments due to stuttering, since at school the words did not come out to me, when I wanted to say something I could not, it was too painful; If I had a job with a colleague and you had to share stories, the damn story didn't come out, nothing came out, I blocked, I stuttered a lot and pufff everything was very complex (in those moments you realize that in many things you need to talk , in everything there is a conversation, short or long in almost everything and thinking that the words do not come out was difficult for me)

I remember that when my mother went to claim the grades she stayed there with the teachers asking them how my speech had gone.They told her that they had chosen me to read in public but that I had cried because of stuttering and that my classmates had laughed .

The truth was that there were many sadnesses and joys because I was always a happy boy regardless of stuttering, I cleared up a lot with my friends, playing, making art, something that was very important to me was creativity, because with it I was able to get out of the world of stuttering and being passionate about art. I really enjoyed making paintings, drawings, dolls, art of all kinds, I had a great time, as well as models, science things, experiments, a lot of things that I enjoyed too much.

When I grew up few things changed, although I felt that stuttering was more and more present, my life was complex because I did not know how to manage stuttering, I always thought that I was different, feeling strange at all times, I thought a lot about: -how the hell The words come out to my colleagues and I do not-

I pass college, I got to university and nothing changed, stuttering began to be a bigger torment in my life. There I thought that it would become of me when I left, what would happen to me, I would really stay all my life stuttering, how could I communicate my ideas, questions came and went constantly, just to lose myself of these questions I thought about other things, but the saddest moments always came these questions.

The career I chose in the university was architecture, the truth was that I had also wanted to study arts, although deep down what I would have wanted most was to study was something that had to do with speaking, because I had always wanted to speak, it was really my passion, but I was very afraid and more than fear it was frustration because I could not do it, I did not imagine myself doing that, nor did it cross my head, it was something like a utopia, a frustrated dream, something that only in another life could I do.

The fact was that I studied architecture, the good This career was that he did not speak much, he did not need to speak, he was simply communicating ideas with drawings, diagrams, models and that's it. It was easy for me, but then you realize that it was all a mask to avoid what you will have to face later.

The first semesters were super good for me, I was the best, I was considered a genius in college. Then as time went by the stuttering got bigger. In the last semesters of architecture my life would change completely, I started to stutter too much, the words did not come out at all, when I saw how my colleagues shared their ideas I kept thinking: -Wow, how can I do that- -I want to speak like him- . I always wanted to be like my colleagues, it was strange to think that everyone admired my talent, but deep down all I wanted was to be like them, to be able to express my ideas freely.

On many occasions, I saw how my classmates would sit next to the teacher and talk to him through some models about the project or idea they had thought of, and when it was my turn, he would deliver a letter saying that I couldn't speak.

160

In the 8th semester and to finish my degree, all my roles were changed, I had been in the faculty quietly since I almost never had to do an exhibition, or expose myself to the public, or talk a lot with my classmates, it was something more than going to class, say hello and leave.

But in this semester everything was different, the teachers had decided that each project should always be exposed to the teacher, what they wanted to say was that each student had to always tell their idea to the teacher and classmates, I as always handed a paper to the teacher explaining my problem with stuttering and the whole thing, but I don't know why this time I had decided not to do it, when it was my turn to expose it was so hard, I would turn red, the words would not come out and I saw how my colleagues looked at me from one so strange way.

In that course you always had to expose the students and teachers, and since I had that dynamic, I went to the classes but I didn't show anything, I just went, then to the final I didn't even go, I just appeared from time to time, because of that guy Of things the teachers began to see that I practically did not go to classes, so that semester I was on the tightrope, but they did not know that I was not going because I was terrified of exposing my stuttering in front of others.

That semester was the most difficult for me, not only because it took me out of my comfort zone but because that semester of architecture was the most complex, I had to be glued to the studio every day to be able to win (literally) so my stress more Knowing that my life had no direction began to link. That semester I don't know why I had promised to speak fluently, I don't know what happened, but I was sick of stuttering, I started watching videos, groups, things here, there, content, but the truth was that nothing gave me that push.

I spend time that semester and things got even worse, every time I saw how it was more difficult to lift the semester since the grades I had were not good, I could only deliver a work at the end of the semester to make it up, I had no more left, and stuttering ufff not to mention, I was thinking about it and getting frustrated… ..until… I met a person in a stuttering group called Caio, this person had written a message in a Facebook group where he said he had a group of stutterers on WhatsApp and that if someone wanted to enter, talk to him. I contacted him and there is something that seemed curious to me, he told me to send him an audio to add me to the group, I thought: what the hell! Does he want to know if I am a stutterer? So I locked myself in the bathroom and opened the WhatsApp app to send an audio and wow-wow-wow I had never sent an audio, it was so weird, so strange, so I said to him choppy ho-ho-ho-la I am … .and I want to… .in-enter the group… he heard this and told me welcome, that I would join the group, I thought he would tell me things about the audio or something like that, and he sent me an audio stuttering a lot, at that moment I I said: wow !! it's like me, I had never been in a relationship with a stutterer, it was so weird, and the weirdest thing was that he sent me stuttering audios, as if he didn't care, I said wow! Well, if the guy has balls to send stuttering audios, I couldn't do that, it was very difficult for me to send him that audio, I remember I sent it in the bathroom locked up with a little voice.

I pass the time and I got to know people in the group, many from there commented on a certain Luismi, who would later become Luis Miguel Morareu. I looked for him on the internet and I realized that he had some videos on YouTube so I started watching them and WOW WOW WOW !! I ate everything he said with potatoes and salsa, WOW WOW !! I had never seen such a way of thinking, from that moment I became obsessed with his videos, I repeated them over and over again. When I entered the WhatsApp group Caio the one that had entered me I used to send audios there constantly, I talked a lot about acceptance, about freely stuttering, that stuttering was a blessing and more things that did not make sense at first, but that later I was finding a very particular meaning.

The days passed and I consumed videos of Luismi while I consumed the audios of Caio, and I was internalizing all this, day after day I consumed everything they said, when I went to university I remember always wearing headphones and listening to Caio's audios and Luismi.

Since that semester I had considered overcoming stuttering or winning the last architecture project, I hoped that one of the two would be successful, indeed, on many occasions I thought about delivering my project with a recording of praise on my part for having overcome stuttering.

162

Weeks passed and everything was fading, I saw how the overcoming of stuttering was lost, and I saw how I sank into the latest architecture project, I thought I was no longer worth anything, everything was disappearing, it was so weird, I felt so sad, stressed, not wanting to live, I began to consider the possibility of losing myself and something else ...

That day to lose myself in the world I contemplated it more and more, it was like a seed that I was creating where I watered it every day, that became more evident than anything else. When the day came to deliver the last architecture project with which I saved the semester, I lost it, although I had done an exceptional project, everyone admired me for that project like the teachers, but the notes that I had accumulated did not give to win the semester , I spoke with the teachers to raise the grade or to see the potential I had but none of that worked.

I got to my house and the next day I left for a distant town, I didn't tell anyone where I was going, I just left, it was sad to leave everything, my family, friends, I don't know what my future would hold, but I left, I thought it had been Everything was a failure, my life had no meaning, how could it have, I had considered overcoming my stuttering or winning the semester and neither of them had left, it was fatal for me.

That day in the town I came to a forest where there were no people, I was alone, with no one, so I sat there all night thinking, thinking ... thinking ... I felt how the cold penetrated my skin, it was the coldest night of all the nights. When I was there I thought about everything: my family, what I had experienced, the things I had done, how everything had happened, I longed for the moments at home ... everything ... How the hell did all this happen? But how? ... questions came and went in that dark solitude.

They spent two days there in that same place and I was thinking so many things, although deep down I always wanted to continue, there is something that told me: hey, the path is still on. I was thinking about stuttering, it was always stuttering, I was thinking if I could defend myself, but then stuttering would come and I was thinking: I don't know, what will I say to others to get a job? How am I going to say things if not the words come out? ...

On the second day I decided to go home again (I skip this part, but all that stuff was very hard, I never thought it would be so hard for my family to have lost me) After this everything became super complex, since, although I had decided not to continue in architecture, they pressured me to get a job and things like that, so I didn't see the green light.

I didn't know what to do, until I thought that what I had to do was get out of my comfort zone, I already had the concepts very well, the Luismi videos learned, I knew very well what Caio had taught me, now I needed to do actions, so I started doing what Luismi once did.

I programmed a daily plan, every day I decided to do something different, and this that I will tell you are the actions that led me to overcome stuttering, before starting with the actions I thought it would be very complex for me to start with things large, so I decided to shorten the objectives, for example I had considered going out and talking with people, but for me to get to talk with people was very far away, so I decided rather to say hello, and so little by little the degree, then one day I thought about going out to the street and saying hello to everyone who passed by me, obviously none of the people I knew but that was my great adventure, to greet everyone no matter what they will say, that day I remember that I I felt super good, it was something I had never done, I knew that if I continued on that path of leaving my comfort zone I would achieve it, the next day I decided to go out and tell people that my name was Santiago and that he accepted me as it was, no It matters if I stuttered or not, what moved me to continue was the adventure of doing it, that day I went out and went to many people, I went to places, shops, everywhere saying: -I am Santiago Rave and I accept myself as I am- the next day I would ask myself the same thing until I felt super comfortable doing that action.

Several days passed where I was interspersed with those actions, I also listened to a lot of inspiring music, all the time, I recorded some affirmations for me where I accepted myself, he said beautiful things to me, he said things that inspired me such as: I am the best, I am a champion, I am a valuable man, I am very big, I don't give a damn what others think, I am worth everything in this life, I am a lion, I had recorded all those statements and had put some background music on them, after I started listening to them daily.

I also remember that every night I wrote down affirmations and the things that I wanted to achieve in a notebook, it was like a planner of my life where I put everything, but there was something that I proposed, that everything I wrote on the planner had to be positive and inspiring . So every night before going to sleep and after getting up I wrote many affirmations, projects, visions, what I hoped to do that day, and all that agenda was a rich fort of inspiration in my life.

Days went by and this time I decided to raise the level of stocks, I went out on the street and spoke hard so that people would listen to me, I went into stores to ask for things that later I did not take, I called all the stores in the telephone directory to make orders that he later canceled, and what seems most curious to me is that people had conversations with me, I remember how I once called to ask about a dog that I was going to buy, obviously I was not going to buy it, this was to get out of my area, I called the store and the very kind man told me what breed I wanted, I told him that I didn't really know which breed and he explained all the breeds he had! the guy wanted to talk and me too, we laughed for a while and it was all very curious, and so I kept calling more and more stores ...

Also in the stuttering group I spoke from time to time with people there to advise them, to guide them, it is something curious because you are supposed to help when you are at the top, but I did not care about that, I knew that I had a long way to go, but I loved to share the road. I also met with several stuttering guys and we shared things. Also in those days I remember there were hard moments where I felt that I was returning, I felt that I was not moving forward, but I continued because I knew that was the way, I had the vision of becoming a great speaker of the world.

I decided to turn up the volume on stocks and started doing all kinds of things like talking on the subway alone, singing on the subway, getting on the buses and talking, I used to take out the phone a lot and pretend I was talking to someone else on the street. another line, but there was no one, only that it gave me reasons to hold conversations in public, I remember that I did that action many times.

I remember a lot when I spoke only in the subway because people kept looking at me like I was crazy or something like that, many times people laughed, and others were angry that they told me to shut up, but I did not do it. It didn't matter a cucumber what the others said. I knew that if I continued on that path I would succeed.

Each time I acquired more and more mental strength, each time I was my best version, each day that passed I proposed a different action. I used to stay at the university for long hours sending audios and conversations on WhatsApp, I sent and sent audios to everyone ... it was a machine to send audios. I also had some books and read, read, read aloud, people even listened and watched as I read, I had proposed with all this to try to enjoy it too, I wanted to enjoy it a lot, I felt that I had to enjoy it.

In those same days, Caio, the one who had joined the group, began to handle certain dynamics or challenges to do, one of them consisted of going out to the street and stuttering with people, something I have to say is that this would be the most important challenge that I would have done. When I decided to do it, I went to university because there were many shops around there and I could enter each one of them to do this dynamic, when I started to do it I began to stutter and exaggerate stuttering, the most curious thing was that people saw me with very calm, I know that deep down they saw it strange because it is not common to see someone stuttering but the reaction of people I thought it would be different, even so if it had been unpleasant I did not give a three as well because I was already very well formed, my mind was in the TOP.

I had thought that people would always judge you or that they would not pay attention to me, but it was the opposite, I saw how in them through the eyes it was reflected all the years that I rejected stuttering and that at that very moment all that was like a ghost that when you touch it vanishes, I had created so much film for several years and at that moment stammering with a person was reduced to nothing, nothing happened, everything was still so normal, it is that the film had been created by me.

I did that several times s with many people because I liked to do things big and when I finished what seemed curious to me was that I stuttered more, I mentioned this dynamic to Caio and he told me that it was normal that he would end up stuttering more, but that later the stuttering would normalize to my normal stuttering, it was as if I created a greater automatism of my stuttering and it learned, then I realized that stuttering was something automatic, it was by learning and that all the rest such as nerves, grief, low self-esteem, the approval of others, were factors that made stuttering soar more and I felt sad, but it was not because of stuttering, it was because of the WAY in which I perceived stuttering, because in that dynamic that I did I felt phenomenal, I think the best dynamic I could have done, an action to remember all my life.

Caio also told me that after this dynamic the stuttering lost more weight and therefore faded more, and so it was, it was something so strange, when I did this action the stuttering increased more because the stuttering exaggerated and therefore my language learned something Again, but at the same time my mind was strengthened in the mental part and then the thoughts were strengthened more making my stuttering later lose weight in my life because she no longer dominated the mental part, and the linguistic part was easier for me to manage, that's why the readings at this point empowered me to another level. And all that was too logical !! Of course!! As my mind already had mental strength, that is, I was a shield with my mind, I took the linguistic part like plasticine because there was no obstacle, before it would have been impossible for me to master it because the mind was consumed by the thoughts I had of the stammering.

The weeks passed and I kept doing more actions, affirmations, speaking, reading, everything really, this is where I started to get my creativity, since I was a child I was always very creative and I felt that if I applied creativity in the process I could overcome stuttering more Quick.

Days passed and I felt much stronger and it was that I began training companies and people, I spoke about happiness, leadership, vision, many companies called me to give them trainings, conferences, everything, I had become a super cool coach I also often had to send emails to companies or foundations to see if they wanted one or another conference, many foundations agreed, some companies also, but I have to say that in many cases I did not receive a response or many others did not want to, I played a lot with the probability, if I sent 100 emails, 5 battlements would say yes or they were in doubt.

I continued with the trainings, talks, and spoke with everyone, I never stopped reading daily, that gave me linguistic strength and I felt that I dominated the word, that I was the best at speaking, I felt great.

Until I began to help people in the WhatsApp group, I entered all the groups that had been and because of stuttering and I began to give my life testimony, the number of people who contacted me daily was impressive, they all wanted to be helped and I I spent hours helping them and advising them on everything, many others contacted me about things that had nothing to do with stuttering, they simply wanted to be inspired, and I also helped them in that, I had become a master of stuttering.

It was then that I decided to create a YouTube channel to help many people, because I received hundreds of emails and messages, I thought that I had to help myself with some tool to be able to reach everyone, since many were left without being able to help, so I started a YouTube channel where I told all my testimony, each process, and helped many through the videos, after that I received many thanks to until today I receive many and many thanks. , and it was a very beautiful stage.

That was basically my overcoming of stuttering, I have to say that in the process there were many more stages, difficult moments, happy moments, moments where I was on the edge, moments where I could not find a way out, many things, like everything in life is a process, nothing is linear, everything is a beautiful roller coaster.

There are many thoughts that are going to happen to you on the way, remember that this is normal, no path is straight, things change when you walk, and let me tell you that this is the wonderful thing about life, that things change, as well as the things change you change, change is possible, I lived it, I felt it, I experienced it in my own flesh, it is real, you know, and that is why I tell you that anyone can do it.

Thanks…

Thank you very much for living this Adventure

Good luck in the Way of Overcoming.

Affirmations

- I LOVE ME AS I AM
- I am a Safe Man
- I am incredibly amazing
- I am the center of attention because I am the best
- When I am doing an exhibition with my colleagues I feel very comfortable, I feel very happy because I am a self-confident man.
- I can talk about all topics calmly with people
- When I am in a conversation I am the one who sets the pace, I am the one who leads the conversation because I understand that I am a man of great value
- I am a man with too much confidence in myself, everything I do I do well, sometimes I am surprised by how great my decisions are.
- I live talking all the time surrounded by people, I talk and talk and my words flow too well, I tell my colleagues about a topic that I like and everyone is interested in my topics and my conversations.
- When I have to make a presentation I do it with so much confidence, I am a very self-confident man, I begin to expose people about the subject that I master and while I present I do it with a smile, very calmly ... I speak too well, while I am exhibiting I look so convincing of who I am, people are fascinated when I expose because I do it better than anyone! I'm the best at it!
- I speak with great confidence and belonging about stuttering because I feel so confident about myself that I don't care what other people think when I talk about stuttering.
- I talk about stuttering and I do it in a very funny way because I know that it is something that gives me a lot of confidence and I feel very good when I talk about stuttering in a funny way.
- The water does not pierce the rock because of its hardness but because of its constancy.

- I feel good when I talk to others
- My words flow like the River
- My voice is Amazing
- I speak with my family with all the confidence and my words touch their hearts.
- I talk to strangers all the time and it is as if I feel like I'm in cotton wool.
- I am there surrounded by people looking into their eyes, talking to them and I feel how each word comes out of my mouth with a lot of energy, my tongue moves throughout my mouth and every sound that comes out I enjoy it and it generates a feeling of tranquility, Peace, I see how all the words come out joining sentences and making my best composition, people see me and listen to me, they look at me, I am the center of attention and I like it a lot !!
- With every word that comes out of my mouth I think: -Wow, how great I speak- I keep talking and I laugh at how wonderful I am when I talk.
- I wake up and can't wait to speak, to get my words out ...
- I talk for long hours and hours and WOWW I enjoy it a lot
- I am an amazing Man when I lead a talk.
- When I speak I feel calm, I love it too much ...
- People understand everything I tell them
- I love when they call me, I stay there for hours talking to people on the phone, I talk and lose track of time, I become the receiver of calls, everyone wants to call me and have a pleasant conversation with me, when they call me and I feel the sound of the phone I feel calm, relax, splendid, I pick up the phone and my words begin to dance one and the other, my voice is charming, then I have a conversation and it is as if I was lying in the clouds, it is like flying over the water and the wind carries me as it carries my lyrics and the harmony of my voice.
- Whenever I communicate I do so with a smile because I know how valuable I am
- My fluency is perfect
- My voice is Amazing
- My words touch people incredibly

• I love to talk, it is what I yearn for the most, every time I pick up my cell phone to send audios I feel a freshness that runs through my entire body and passes through my stomach until it reaches my neck where my mouth cords start to vibrate and I feel very well! It is a very intense feeling of freshness that tells me that it is wonderful to send audios, I love so much to send audios to my colleagues, friends, families, I keep sending audios for hours, and I talk about my life, my hobbies, what I do. Passionate about the things that I like to do and travel, I dream big and I love talking.

• I love talking to people

• I feel comfortable when I chat with others

• I chat with many people about new ideas

• I am very comfortable exposing to crowds of people

• I look people in the eye when I say anything because I know that deep down I am a self-confident man and I trust myself and I know that what other people think about me I don't give a shit and three hectares of shit

• People understand everything I speak to them, through my lungs I receive the essence of air and it circulates freely through my lungs mm-mmm, I receive all the air with energy and gratitude and all my muscles are fresh and relaxed and I feel like the air passes through my larynx touches my vocal cords and they begin to vibrate with energy and my words come out s resounding splendidly like happiness… I love to vibrate with my words and that my voice is the best!

• I feel good when I convey my words

• I am a Safe Man

• I feel so happy when I express myself, I have a lot of fun.

• I meet new people and talk to them in a calm, relaxed way about what I like.

• Wow my verbal fluency is perfect !!

• I am a Unique man !!

• When I speak my words begin to turn into sweet tones that inspire people.

• My speech is the best in the world.

• I feel calm and relaxed

• My breathing is continuous

• I am a very strong man because that is my only option.

• I see others as ants because I am bigger than everyone

- The world knows and will know how great I AM
- I am a very Courageous man
- I have the possibility to do what I want because my mind has all the possibilities
- I am a God to speak
- I know and I only know that I am the most important person in the world
- I love myself and there is no one who loves himself as I do, that is why I see others as very small
- My ego is so big that he tells me that I am the best at everything I do and that when I speak I am the best at it
- When I have an exhibition I go out there and show how valuable I am because I know that there is no one better than me at doing exhibitions
- I am very clear that what others think matters to me three cucumbers because I am the only one who gives me value and validity, always me and only me, that is why I do well in everything I do.
- My self-esteem is through the roof because the clouds are what defines me there, I always like to touch the sky with my hands, for that reason I always put my self-esteem at the top since that is me and it makes me unique and better than anyone.
- I don't give a shit what they think of me
- I don't give a shit I always do what I want
- I am an impressive man
- I dazzle when I speak and when I express myself I am fascinating
- I am worth more than gold
- I am infinitely Big
- I only approve myself, always me
- In this life I am and will be the best
- The game is always over when I WIN
- When I expose I know and I have but it is very clear that what others think I pass through the balls
- I have a tattoo on my mind that I don't give a damn what they think of me
- My word is strong because I have a firm footing
- I am Powerful and Safe
- I am a Being of Temple because I am a Great soldier who fights in the best battles

- What people think I don't care about three hectares of shit
- In this life I do and will do whatever I please
-       I am incredible
- I do things thinking of myself and not of others because on the day of my death I want people to know that I did what made my balls swell and I was very happy.
- On my tombstone I would like you to say here lies a man who knew how to value himself and who did not pay attention to others.
- I am a Being Sure of myself
- I LOVE ME THOROUGHLY
- I always do everything I do well.
- I don't need anyone's approval to know how Big I am.
- I am a very confident man
- I always choose my own path: my happiness
- I always do what I say and if I say I don't give a shit what other people think it is!
- I just enjoy everything
- When I talk to people I only think about contributing to them because after what they think I throw it away
- I live to my fullest potential
- I am a prosperous man
- I am an executor who always does the actions
- I am a very confident Leader
- Every day I am more sure of myself
- I feel like a great Leader
- I know that I deserve this life
- I get everything I think and what I speak
- I am a God of speech and I expose like no one else
- It is me and always me because I know that I will always be with me
- I always attract the best moments to give myself more Value
- Confidence is my second nature because the first is my greatness
- I always believe in myself
- My actions are safe, they bring me closer to my goals and I am an excellent man
- I do everything I do with excellence
- I make the best contributions to people since I am the best at what I speak

174

• I know that many people love me and others hate me, those who love thank you very much and those who hate me also because they advertise me for free and it is better that they talk about me because I am important
• I love and accept myself unconditionally
• The thanks to the crops, the criticisms I build them and the opinions of the people I pass them with toilet paper.
• I always see the best of me
• I always move towards the direction of my strength and my self-esteem in heaven because I am a God for speaking.
• I don't give a shit what other people think of me because I'm worth everything
• I am infinitely BIG

Schedule Annex
1) Affirmations visualizations every morning
2) Write A and B: A in past form and B in Future, then in present.
3) language changes.
4) Readings modulated 1 hour of books "see you as the Best"
5) Phrases on the cell phone and desk.
6) Positive music.

7) Create the claims themselves

8) Plan Drawing

9) Schedule of consulting dates

10) Stock Plan

By the Author of the best Latin Book on Stuttering

Rave Herrera

Correct Stuttering

Discover the power to Transform your life

RAVE

Made in United States
North Haven, CT
02 December 2022

27701076R00107